She Blooms

She Blooms

finding home after the convent

A MEMOIR

Maura Doherty

WHITE RIVER PRESS

Copyright 2024 by Maura Doherty
All rights reserved.

Published by White River Press, Amherst, Massachusetts
whiteriverpress.com

ISBN: 979-8-88545-014-0

Book and cover design by I Libri Book Design

LIBRARY OF CONGRESS CATALOGING-IN-PUBLICATION DATA
Names: Doherty, Maura Bridget, 1949– author.
Title: She blooms : finding home after the convent : a memoir / Maura Doherty.
Description: Amherst, Massachusetts : White River Press, [2024]
Identifiers: LCCN 2024009233 | ISBN 9798885450140 (paperback)
Subjects: LCSH: Doherty, Maura Bridget, 1949– | Ex-nuns—United States—Biography. | LCGFT: Autobiographies.
Classification: LCC BX4668.3.D64 A3 2024 | DDC 282.092 [B]–dc23/eng/20240612
LC record available at https://lccn.loc.gov/2024009233

AUTHOR'S NOTE

This is a work of nonfiction. Characters and scenes are based in reality, although some dates and names have been altered and dialogue created to allow for narrative flow.

PHOTO CREDITS

author photo: Ed Celnicker
gardenia: juicybits | iStock
rosary: Weigand | Photocase
tree of life: artdock | Shutterstock

*To my parents, Francis and Kathleen Tivnan Doherty,
and all the mentors who helped me bloom.*

contents

PART I ◆ Before

CHAPTER 1   Am I Good Enough?   *3*
CHAPTER 2   Sisters   *7*
CHAPTER 3   Home   *21*
CHAPTER 4   The Decision   *35*

PART II ◆ During

CHAPTER 5   Novitiate   *49*
CHAPTER 6   Easter   *93*
CHAPTER 7   Teaching   *99*
CHAPTER 8   Alpha House   *105*
CHAPTER 9   Aquinas High School   *121*
CHAPTER 10   Turning Points   *133*
CHAPTER 11   From the Coffin   *149*

Photographs   *159*

PART III ✦ After

CHAPTER 12 First Boyfriend *175*
CHAPTER 13 Work *183*
CHAPTER 14 Ireland *189*
CHAPTER 15 Highlander Center *199*
CHAPTER 16 Bumpass Cove *219*
CHAPTER 17 Slaying Dragons *233*

PART IV ✦ Stories, Not Secrets

CHAPTER 18 I Didn't Have a Seizure *257*
CHAPTER 19 Bloom *279*

Epilogue *287*

Acknowledgments *291*

part one

Before

TRINITY KNOT
HOME ✦ MAURA ✦ CHURCH

one

AM I GOOD ENOUGH?

NOT EVERY GIRL makes a vow of chastity or obedience. Not many girls make a deal to live within the confines of a convent and to follow rules every single day for the rest of her life. How about a vow of poverty? Know any girls who go looking for that?

I knew one: Me.

This is my story.

IT WAS 1967. I was kneeling in a choir stall, head lowered. My short postulant veil slipped back a few inches on my head as if it knew I was new at this. I was. I was eighteen. The summer heat of Rockland County, New York, covered my face and arms with sweat.

Am I good enough to be a nun?

Sister Mary Doreen was on my left. Her dark brown bangs almost reached her eyebrows. Maybe if I had bangs, my veil wouldn't slide. She loved to study philosophy and theology. Books about Kant or Teilhard de Chardin sat on the handle of the dust mop as she walked up and down the marble halls.

Me? I studied, but not like her. I just wanted to get through college and teach high school. As she turned and smiled, her glasses caught the dim glow from lights overhead. It was 6:00 a.m. Too early for kneeling in a sweltering chapel at the motherhouse of the Dominican Sisters in Sparkill, a small hamlet west of the Hudson River.

A dozen novices clad in white from head to toe sat across the chapel. Sister Margaret Gerard, our Postulant Mistress, frowned when she declared, "Never talk to the novices. They're in a year of prayer and meditation before they take final vows."

The novices got the privilege of wearing the long white habit, like the ones that the Sisters who taught me wore. But the novices had white veils, not black.

Two dozen of my fellow first-year nuns (we were called postulants) sat around me, black veils all in a row. Short capes flared over our elbows and hovered over our calf-length dresses. We were all in black, like crows. But, unlike crows, we were silent. Maybe some were as nervous as I was. But I didn't know. We weren't allowed to talk.

Mary's head was still bowed. Was she praying? When she snorted, I realized she was sleeping. Lucky her. I couldn't nap while I was half prone on a choir bench. Not with the eyes of the nuns in white watching me from across the aisle. Then there were dozens of professed nuns in pews around the chapel. A bell echoed; Mary startled and stood with the rest of us.

One of the novices chanted the opening of *Lauds* in Latin. "Deus, in adiutórium meum intende."

The rest of us intoned the response. "Domine, ad adiuvándum me festina."

When we finished chanting and sat down to meditate, I found the translation in *The Divine Office* prayer book:

O God, come to our aid.
O Lord, make haste to help us.

Tears welled up and threatened to spill over. Will God help me become a good nun? Dad used to tell me to do my best. One day, I waited for him to praise me after I showed him my math test. Instead of congratulating me he said, "You only got an A? Why not an A+?"

My heart hurt. "Dad, an A is a great grade."

"You can always do better, Maura. Try for an A+ next time."

My joy fled as I took the paper from his hand.

Will the convent be like that? A place where I wouldn't feel like I was good enough? In the chapel, I pressed my hands together and pled to a God I barely knew. *O, God, help me.* I hoped I could be a good Sister. I wanted to ace my time in this place they called the novitiate. I wanted to be the best nun ever.

Two

SISTERS

I GREW UP with four brothers—Francis, four years older; John, two years younger; Michael, three years younger; and Peter, six years younger than me—and two sisters—Jo Anne, a year younger than me, and Colleen, two years older. Colleen always seemed to know what to do. Her long brown hair curled just right. She had lots of phone calls from girlfriends, filled with her whispering and laughing as she sat on the couch in the cramped TV room. She talked and talked until Dad threatened to "put a lock on the phone." Jo Anne would slip out of the house to go places I never heard about. Me? I kept to myself and studied.

I had other Sisters, too—the ones who taught me in school who wore long white dresses and black veils. Sister Catherine Mary taught me in kindergarten. She was even taller than Dad, and he was really tall. When she helped me with my work, she had to lean way down to reach my book. She smiled a lot and when she did, her cheeks got pink like when Mom put on makeup, but Sister's cheeks got pink when she smiled. When her finger traced the blue sky and green grass in my drawing, I wanted to be in the picture with her, holding her hand. I bet her hand would be soft, so soft I wouldn't want to let it go.

In second grade I had Sister Dennis Martin who played with us in the schoolyard. She ran faster than anyone and jumped high to catch the ball. She had to hold her dress and rosary beads so she wouldn't trip. My uniform was shorter than hers, so I didn't have to do that.

The first time I saw the Sisters in school, I wasn't afraid of them. Patricia, who sat in front of me, cried because she thought they looked scary—they were covered in black and white so all we could see were Sister's face and hands. And they had the longest rosary beads I'd ever seen—way longer than the ones Mom prayed with. Why wasn't I afraid? Because our family had two Sisters who looked a little like the ones in school—Cousin Mary and Aunt Jo.

Cousin Mary wore a poofy black dress with little rosary beads and a funny black cap that covered her hair. She was Dad's cousin. Her parents were Irish and when they talked, their accents sounded like my parents. Her mother was my godmother. Years later Mary told me, "Your father lived with us when he first came over from Ireland. He cleaned and cooked for us and helped my sister and me with our studies. He knew all about math and Latin. He showed me how to figure everything out. He was so smart!"

I knew Dad was smart but he cleaned and cooked? Mom does that, not Dad.

I don't think Aunt Jo or Cousin Mary played ball like Sister Dennis Martin. Seven-year-old me, head down, always worried that Sister Dennis Martin would be mad if I didn't understand my homework assignment. But she never was. She just leaned over and quietly explained to me how to complete the work. When I looked up, she smiled. And I knew I was okay.

Mom had a photo of Aunt Jo before she entered the convent on the mantlepiece in the front room. She looked a lot like Mom with long brown hair. She wore a green high-necked dress that looked fancy and matched her dark brown eyes.

The trip to visit Aunt Jo meant a long drive to Boston. Dad drove because Mom didn't drive. Years later she told me, "Driving made me too nervous."

When I was seven, we all packed into Dad's car to go see Aunt Jo. Jo Anne and I sat on the floor in back, three of our brothers and Colleen were on the back seat, and one-year-old Peter was in the front on Mom's lap. I loved sitting on the floor. It was a little spot just for me in my favorite butterfly dress with everyone squished around me.

Would Aunt Jo look like her picture on the mantle? No. She, she was a nun now. She'll look like the Sisters in school. Right?

Dad had to pull over a lot because we had to use the bathroom. Hours later when we got to Aunt Jo's, there was a big statue of a man in the middle of the driveway. He had on a long robe and a little stone bird perched on one of his outstretched hands. I wondered how the bird got there and if it ever got to fly away.

When we got out of the car, Mom lined us up, pulled her fingers through us girls' hair, hoisted up socks, and straightened our dresses. My butterfly dress looked pretty when I twirled around in the sunlight. Dad tucked in John and Michael's shirts since they were only five- and four-years-old, and ran a comb through their hair. Francis, all of eleven, combed his hair and tucked in his own shirt. Mom went up the steps with one-year-old Peter asleep in her arms. Next came my sisters, Colleen, nine years old; and Jo Anne, six; and me, seven; then Dad with the boys in front of him. My stomach rolled a little when I climbed those steps as if the butterflies on my dress wanted me to fly away with them. I held my breath when Mom pulled open the door.

Inside it was quiet, so quiet it was kind of spooky because no one was there. It was a big open place with a shiny white floor that made our shoes sound real loud. One corner had statues of the Infant of Prague like the one we had back home.

Mom brought us over to the wall, only it wasn't just a wall because it had a doorbell and a sign that read "THE TURN." When she rang the doorbell, it sounded like ours back home. Now my stomach was buzzing like all the butterflies were flying around inside me. Then someone answered Mom from inside the wall! They said something about God and welcome and something else I don't remember.

Mom pushed her head real close to the wall and said, "It's Kathleen Doherty and family for Sister Mary Columba." Then she told the wall she had some things for Aunt Jo and the Sisters. Like magic, the wall opened, and Mom put an apple pie and other things on shelves inside the lazy Susan turntable, then said, "All right, Sister," and it disappeared behind the wall! I forgot about my stomach and butterflies and watched everything go away. I could have watched it again and again, but Mom took my hand and led us down the hall to the room where we could see Aunt Jo. John and Michael tried to run down the hall, but Dad held their hands so they stayed close and didn't cry or anything like they did at home.

Mom said we were supposed to be quiet because Aunt Jo prayed a lot. Mom should know because Aunt Jo was her sister. Her name was Jo for Josephine, and Jo Anne was named after her. But because nuns needed special holy names, Aunt Jo was also called Sister Mary Columba. When we walked down the hall and into the room, everyone's shoes were loud, but I could hear my shoes the best because they were my Sunday shoes. The floor was so shiny I could almost see my reflection in it, except Mom made us go so fast I didn't get to look at it too long.

Mom walked into a room, turned on the lights, and pulled up chairs in front of a large window with a metal screen that had wooden shutters behind it. Where was Aunt Jo? A few minutes later I heard something soft, like someone was walking on tiptoes like I do sometimes, and the shutters swung open. Who was this? I hopped off my chair and hid behind Mom. This person wore a long brown dress and a white thing that covered her hair and a black veil, kind of like the Sisters at school, only different.

Mom said, "Everyone, this is Aunt Jo." I peeked out from behind Mom, and there was Aunt Jo, smiling at me.

She leaned close to the screen and said, "Hello," so quiet, like how I told Jo Anne a secret. But Aunt Jo talked like Mom and Dad in an Irish voice. Instead of the rosary beads like the Sisters wore in school, she had a rope with knots around her waist. It looked like the rope off the back porch that Mom used to hang clothes, only Mom's rope didn't have knots in it like Aunt Jo's. Aunt Jo wasn't in the room with us; she was in the next room and the metal screen was between us. It was not like the screen that keeps out bugs but thicker, one that would keep her inside. Mom said she was in a special place called a cloister and couldn't come to the Bronx to see us. That was why we had to go see her in the cloister in Boston.

⟡

MY FAVORITE VISIT to see Aunt Jo was when I was thirteen when just the girls went. We took an Amtrak train to Boston and then a taxi and spent two nights in the guest room at the monastery. It was the first time I took a train and a taxi and stayed in a monastery! The train was fun because I could look out the window and watch all the people and cars in the towns along the way. Mom brought sandwiches and said we could go to the dining car and buy milk for us and a coffee for her. Colleen and I walked down the aisles of several cars and through all the doorways as the train moved along the track. Sometimes it jumped around and I had to hold on to the seats so I didn't fall.

When we got to the dining car, Colleen asked a man in a red jacket, "May we have one coffee and three orders of milk, please?"

"Yes, madam. Coming right up."

Colleen was only fifteen but sounded grown up and looked it, too. She was a few inches taller than I was, and her dark brown hair was curled in a perfect page boy. Her plaid jumper even matched the red and white curtains on the windows. It was like she belonged there and knew what to do. I didn't feel like that. I was worried we might spill Mom's coffee on our way back to our seats. But that didn't happen. We got back to our seat, ate sandwiches, and drank our milk. I closed my eyes and felt the rumble of the train as it went down the track.

When we got to Boston, we picked up our suitcases and shopping bags and walked out of the station. Mom led us to the sidewalk where she raised her arm to call a cab. One came right away, and the driver helped us put everything in the trunk.

Mom told the driver, "Please take us to 920 Centre Street in Jamaica Plain. It's the Franciscan Monastery of the Poor Clare."

He responded, "Of course, madam." And started the meter running.

I knew we were close when we passed Jamaica Pond and pulled into the circular driveway with the statue of Saint Francis (I knew his name by then) with the bird on his outstretched finger. Mom paid the driver and we picked up our bags. I felt older and wiser as I mounted the front steps. I'd come a long way to get here.

Just like on other visits, Mom rang the doorbell by "The Turn," and told the Sister behind the wall who we were. This time, when I heard Sister say, "Please go to parlor two," I knew what to do. I picked up a suitcase and walked down the hall, listening to the tap, tap, tap of my heels on the waxed floor before I entered the room, turned on the lights, stowed the suitcase in the corner of that beige and brown stucco parlor, and pulled four straight back chairs in front of the metal screen.

Within a few minutes Aunt Jo opened the shutters behind the screen that separated us. She stood up as close as she could, said hello, and smiled; when she did, her cheeks lifted and her eyes glinted in the overhead light. She looked like a younger version of my mother. I was used to how she looked by now and noticed how her smile lit up the room, not like a blazing sun but more like a slow, warm sunrise, joyful and loving all at once.

Mom had seven children and didn't smile much. Aunt Jo

had God and no children, and she smiled. Her Irish brogue, along with her cloister-whisper voice, made it difficult for me to hear what she was saying unless I pulled my chair close to the screen next to Mom. Mom and Aunt Jo's Irish accents were called a brogue. I thought it was strange that an Irish accent went by a name for a shoe. I never saw Aunt Jo's shoes because of her long habit.

I got used to looking at Aunt Jo through that screen each time we visited in spite of the image of her being partly blocked by the metal. The openings in the screen were big enough for my aunt to fit her fingers through. First, her index finger, then, one by one, her middle, ring, and pinky fingers, rubbing the edge of the openings in the metal, as if it helped her relax, as if it brought her closer to us.

"Joe McDonagh is over his pneumonia, thanks be to God." Aunt Jo stroked the metal with a slender index finger with rough cuticles. As she spoke, her eyes filled with something I didn't understand. Was it worry? Or love?

Joe McDonagh? Who's he? Is he related to Mom's cousin, Kathleen McDonagh?

"Ah, that's good, Jo." Mom nodded, upright in the straight-backed chair as her sister caressed the screen that separated their worlds. Mom's short-sleeved, brown-and-white dress seemed festive against the neutral tones of the visiting room. She smelled like the powder she used for special occasions, the air around her filled with a hint of springtime sweetness.

"Kathleen hopes to visit him this summer."

We call Kathleen McDonagh the funny lady because she's always laughing. She has a big face and isn't pretty, but she's always happy. Maybe Joe is her brother?

"The Tivnan cousins write me as well. Joseph uses a cane because of his arthritis."

Tivnan cousins? Joseph Tivnan? I didn't know about them either.

As Aunt Jo talked the wide sleeves of the brown wool habit revealed a slender arm covered in a long-sleeved white T-shirt as she poked another finger through the opening in the metal screen. "He's still a rascal, Kathleen. He reminded me of the day we all played hooky and rode our bikes over to the strand."

Mom and Aunt Jo laughed. The air in the bare visiting parlor brightened as they shook their heads remembering their childhood in Ireland. I didn't know then that to my Irish family, a strand referred to the beach. In any case, it sounded more fun than going to school. And I wanted to meet Joseph Tivnan.

Mom's shoulders relaxed as she talked to Aunt Jo. I was a teenager, mesmerized by the flow of words between these two women, the familiarity they had, how they cared for each other and the family they'd left behind in Ireland. This was different than listening to Mom in the kitchen as she talked with her friend, Mrs. Slevin. This was a revelation, this miracle of conversation flowing from one sister to another. This was about family, about Ireland, something Mom didn't talk about with me or any of us. At one point Mom turned to my sisters and me. "Why don't you girls go outside? Just stay close to the front entrance."

I didn't want to leave that room, but Mom narrowed her eyes at me until I stood up and followed Colleen and Jo Anne into the hallway. Our leather heels tapped on the polished marble floor as sunlight streamed through windows that looked out on the front lawn. As I walked, I peered into three more parlors, all waiting for families to visit. The main lobby was empty. "The Turn" waited for the next delivery, perhaps another pie or family photos like the ones Mom had left. The glass display case on the far wall drew me closer. Three statues of the Infant of Prague in flowing satin robes sat on the shelf—one white, one red, one blue, and all embroidered with tiny roses. Had Aunt Jo made them? She had sent us one that Mom put on the mantlepiece in the front room. Mom changed the robes depending on the season—white for most of the year, red for July for the Sacred Heart, and blue in May to honor Mary. Standing at the display case now, I decided I liked the red one best, just as Colleen called out.

"Maura, come on. We need to go outside." Her impatience echoed across the lobby as she spoke in her "I'm older than you, you'd better come now" voice.

"I'm coming." As I went down the front steps, I saw Jo Anne running around the circular driveway with the statue of Saint Francis in the middle.

"You can't catch me, Maura."

I ran after her, laughing and panting as she raced around the statue. Then she darted over to the rose bushes along the front of the building—red roses, like the ones Mom grew at home, the ones with a strong fragrance. I slowed down to smell them and thought about Mom and Aunt Jo. *What were they saying now? What had I missed? Had Mom been like me when she was my age? Did she have fun?*

Just then, Jo Anne screamed and ran out of the bushes on the other side of the driveway. A swarm of what looked like wasps were all around her. Colleen and I ran over, waved them away, and pulled her up the front steps and into the lobby.

Jo Anne was crying so loud that Mom ran into the hallway to see what had happened. Jo Anne was covered in stings, red blisters that covered much of her face, legs, and arms. A Sister came out the side door.

"I'm Sister Loretta, the extern Sister. Let me help you. Will you come with me?" We followed her into the guest dining room across the hall, with Jo Anne whimpering in pain the whole time. "I have something that will help," Sister Loretta said. "Just give me a minute." She left, and in a couple of minutes she came back with a dish filled with a white paste. "Baking soda and water. One of the best remedies for stings." Mom held Jo Anne as Sister applied the paste all over the stings. The ones on Jo Anne's lip and ear had swollen up. It looked like little marshmallows were under her skin trying to get out. But Jo Anne was still in pain, so Sister Loretta and Mom wiped her all over with a warm face cloth before they brought her to bed. Colleen and I followed.

"Oh, Jo Anne, these will go down in a couple of days, but not yet," Sister said. "Let's put more baking soda on her. Do you agree, Mrs. Doherty?"

Mom nodded and held Jo Anne's hand as Sister Loretta made up more of her remedy. I felt sorry for my younger sister, so far from home and in such pain. The good news was that by the time we left to go home, Jo Anne felt a little better and her face and skin weren't so swollen.

One of the best things about this visit was staying in the monastery's guest rooms, which were in a wing outside the cloister. Jo Anne and I shared one room, and Mom and Colleen shared another. It was like hiding out in the monastery without needing to go to church.

Peace emanated from my aunt and the Sisters who made

us feel at home in that strange place. Over the next several years, Aunt Jo became a gateway for me, to my mother's family in Grange, County Sligo, Ireland, and much later, to my own vocation. Stepping into the monastery allowed me to enter a world where peace reigned. The quiet astounded me. My reality shifted. I felt different. Nothing like Maura from the crowded home back on Olmstead Avenue. I was softer, kinder, like I could let go of the hurts and disappointments I'd felt as third from the top and fifth from the bottom in the roster of seven children. Perhaps here, where I held my breath each time Aunt Jo came into view from behind that screen, I not only beheld my aunt but a glimmer of myself—Maura Bridget Clare Doherty, hopeful, radiant, and intrigued by the mystery that filtered out from within the monastery walls. It was a mystery I wanted to know more about, one that drew me in. My aunt and her fellow Sisters knew something I didn't. The cloistered life didn't appeal to me, but I wanted to know why Aunt Jo looked so happy, so at home. This was something I hadn't encountered before. Years later, when I was in high school and saw Sister Perpetua's glowing face, I remembered Aunt Jo. Her peace. Her joy.

And I wanted it for myself.

AS A CHILD, God meant going to church, being quiet, not poking the friend, brother, or sister who sat next to me on the hard oak pew. It meant listening to the man called a priest who wore long gold gowns and spoke Latin. I did what the Sisters told me to do, but it didn't mean anything except that I wanted to be good so Sister would like me. I didn't like the priest since most of the time he had his back to me when he spoke. As I got older, the Sisters told me what the Latin words meant.

The priest would say, "Dominus Vobiscum," and we'd reply, "Et cum spiritu tuo."

What he'd said translated to English as, "God be with you." And we'd answer, "And with your spirit."

Now I know these were wonderful wishes. *May the spirit of love be with you. May your spirit be filled with love.* Back then, this didn't occur to me. I was a child parroting what I was told to say in church, an austere place with a crucifix hung over the altar. The crucifix showed a man tortured to death, hung for all to see him in his crown of thorns. As a child, I didn't see that. I saw that God loved me so much he sent his son to die for my sins.

Later, much later, I was drawn to the mysterious world of spirit and spirituality. Not to the priests who ruled the Mass, but to the Sisters who cared for each other and the world around them. These Sisters believed in God and goodness and love. I wanted what they had.

But that was much later.

three

HOME

AFTER WE GOT back from Boston, Mom fixed dinner. She sat at the end of the kitchen table eating a miniscule piece of chicken and a boiled potato. Francis, Michael, John, and Peter shoved food into their mouths like they were in a race. John held a fork in one hand and pinched Michael under the table with his other hand. I saw him when I reached down to chase a pea that had shot off my plate.

"Sister Jerome fell asleep again in Algebra class," fifteen-year-old Colleen said as she finished eating a potato. Twelve-year-old Jo Anne's eyes popped open. I was two years younger than Colleen but I didn't believe her, even though she looked serious when she said this. My eighth-grade teacher, Sister Boniface, *never* fell asleep in class. She kept her eyes glued to every student in our classroom.

The Sisters who taught in both my grammar school and Colleen's high school were from the same community of Sisters. Sister Dennis Martin was my favorite. Her smile lit up the classroom. Sister Boniface, however, never smiled.

The clock on the wall clicked out the seconds. After Mom

swallowed the last of her dinner, she took a drag from an Old Gold cigarette. The picture of the Sacred Heart looked down on me from the corner altar with its red votive light casting a soft glow over my head. Dad was late from his extra job as a security guard, which meant that when he got home, he'd be too tired to look over my homework. Maybe he could quiz me before the next spelling test. Maybe.

"Mom, can I help wash the dishes?" I loved the soap Mom got from the A&P on Castle Hill Avenue. It made lots of bubbles and made the job fun.

"No, Maura. Just leave it and let me have some peace."

Everyone left so Mom could clean up. She never wanted help—not even though there were seven of us and only one of her. The crucifix on the wall overhead loomed over me as I got up from the table. I wondered if Jesus wasn't happy that I left all the work for Mom.

My parents owned the duplex at 1210 Olmstead Avenue in the Bronx where we lived on the first floor and rented out the upstairs apartment. The front room was reserved for company; it connected to the girls' bedroom next to the TV room where my parents slept on a pull-out couch. The kitchen, boys' bedroom, TV room, and bathroom faced a short hall off an outer hallway that led to the front door and the stairs to the upstairs apartment. Eight brick steps went down from a front porch to the sidewalk where dozens of children played "running bases," freeze tag, and jump rope. Our home was just a few houses away from the rumble of six lanes of traffic on the Cross Bronx Expressway. I was surrounded by the screech of brakes, the thrum of wheels on asphalt, and the constant clamor of children. I hungered for quiet.

The kitchen was Mom's domain. She spent much of her

time cooking, cleaning, and sitting at the kitchen table sipping coffee and smoking—her kind of peace didn't include having us too close. The kitchen had a door to the back porch with two clotheslines where Mom hung out wet wash year-round. It overlooked a yard where Dad barbecued hot dogs and Mom grew roses and tomatoes in summer.

After dinner I walked through the TV room into the girls' bedroom. My bed was part of a high-riser and was stored under Colleen's bed during the day. Jo Anne's bed was on the wall across from Colleen's.

"Don't sit on my bed," Colleen warned when I began to sit down, my legs leaning against the edge of the pink bedspread. Across the small room, Jo Anne was busy arranging her dolls against her pillow. I went back to the TV room and sat on the couch as questions ran through my mind. *Why did Dad have to work so much? Why was Mom tired all the time?*

Mom went past the open doorway, grabbed a broom from the outer hall, and walked back to the kitchen without a glance at me or the *Reader's Digest* open on my lap. Smoke filtered my way as I heard the scrape of broom across the kitchen floor. I think cigarettes helped save Mom. But saved her from what?

I sat still as I heard the dustpan bang against linoleum, followed by crumbs being swept up then dumped in the garbage. The sound of running water was followed by the acrid odor of ammonia and the swish of wet mop. Soon she'd dump the contents of the bucket down the sink, rinse and wring out the mop, and stow it on the back porch. I heard her open the back door and, in a few minutes, I knew she'd return to her chair in the TV room a few feet from me.

I tucked the magazine under my arm and walked back through the girls' bedroom. Colleen was lying on her bed with her eyes closed; Jo Anne was sitting on her own bed, curling the hair of her Shirley Temple doll with a small brush. Neither of my sisters looked at me as I pushed open the door to the front room, the one reserved for guests and the Christmas tree and my brothers' Lionel train set. I closed the door and took a few steps. The beige and maroon rug was soft under my Keds. When I turned it on, Aunt Jo's hurricane lamp cast a soothing glow to the room. Its glass globe was decorated with delicate pink flowers. The radiator clicked out heat even though I had goosebumps from the chill around me. Even the roar of traffic from the Cross Bronx Expressway seemed muted here.

Aunt Jo would love this room. The photograph of her before she entered the convent graced the top of the mantle next to the statue of the Infant of Prague dressed in a white satin robe. Aunt Jo's hair fell in soft waves around her face. She always smiled when we visited her in the monastery, her Irish brogue so much like Mom's, her face more slender, yet so like Mom's, too. As I looked at her picture, my chest tightened. I wasn't supposed to be in the front room. A quick look out the bay windows told me that going outside wasn't an option. February rain was blowing sideways and pellets of ice were hitting the windows as if they wanted in. But Mom wouldn't think to look for me here. My breathing eased.

Dad's photo was placed on the other side of the Infant of Prague. He looked young and handsome in his Army cap and uniform, with no evidence of the positive test for tuberculosis that later merited him an early discharge. A painting of Ben Bulben—which we always called "Mom's Mountain"—sat to the right of his photo. Its steep hillsides overlooked Mom's hometown of Grange, County Sligo, and, beyond that, the Atlantic Ocean.

What was Mom's home like in Ireland? Was it like ours? Someday, I promised myself. *Someday I'll visit that mountain.* I didn't know how I'd get there, but I tucked that promise away like a secret.

I looked down to the fake logs in the fireplace with the crook and crane that Uncle Jimmy, Aunt Maggie's husband, the blacksmith, had made. Aunt Maggie was Dad's sister. The crook was a hook that held a large cast iron pot. Years later, Aunt Maggie told me Mom had one just like it in Ireland.

I wasn't brave enough to turn on the light for the fake flames behind the logs. Just being here, a room reserved for special company, was enough of a risk. I looked past the armchair to the small shelves on either side of the door to the girls' bedroom. A small, framed photo of a woman in a long, flowing blue dress and matching wide brimmed hat sat on the lower shelf. Who was she? The man at her side stood at attention, his handlebar mustache dark against his pale skin. *Were they relatives? Mom's parents? And why didn't I know?*

Once, when I asked Mom about Ireland, she said, "Maura, that's all in the past. We're Americans now."

I noticed two cabinets under the shelves that held that photo. How had I not noticed them before? I waited. There were no sounds from my sisters in the bedroom next door. Only the faint sound of a television that told me Mom was sitting in her chair in the TV room. I leaned down and pulled on the handle of the first cabinet. The door was stuck. I pulled harder, and it popped open with a thunk. I caught my breath. No one came to see what I was up to. The second cabinet opened without a struggle. Books! Both cabinets had books in them. I had no idea we had books behind those closed doors.

It wasn't as if I didn't have books. I had schoolbooks and library books, and my parents had bought us a set of children's encyclopedias. But these books were different. They looked less boring, more grown-up. I flipped through the first one—there weren't any pictures. Then I picked out another one, walked to the couch, sat down, and started to read. At first, I couldn't follow the story. Something about a beautiful woman who wore hoop dresses and lived on a plantation. The title was *Gone with the Wind*. I got so engrossed that when I looked up it was dark outside. Mom might have missed me by now, so I marked the page, put the book back in the cabinet, left the front room, and went back to the bedroom. Colleen was still lying on the bed, eyes open now. Jo Anne was changing the dress on her Betsy Wetsy doll. I took a breath and walked into the TV room. Mom was asleep in the chair, the TV tuned to a show about telling the truth. Tendrils of smoke wafted from the cigarette in the ashtray on the side table. I tiptoed past her, went into the kitchen, took a piece of loose-leaf paper from a package that always sat on the counter, and started to draw Tara, home of Scarlett of the voluminous skirts, from the story hidden in the cabinet. I started with the columns on the mansion that was even bigger than our family could fill; I penciled in a massive front door and dozens of windows. I chose the room at the top of the house as mine and decorated its curtains with polka dots. I imagined it filled with lots of books and a couch of my own. My safe place, one I didn't have to share with my siblings. In that moment my spirits lifted, transforming the whiff of ammonia that surrounded me in the kitchen into the fragrance of magnolias—Scarlett's favorite flower, one I'd never seen but imagined to be as beautiful as she was. It didn't matter that the book made little sense, that I knew little about many of the words that were passed back and forth between characters, including the slaves who did all the work. But I did understand that Scarlett wore an impossibly big skirt, had a strong personality, and lived in a home called Tara.

Wasn't Tara an Irish name?

One day, I promised myself, I'd find out more about women like Scarlett who didn't care what others thought. *Someday.* Until then I returned the book to the forbidden front room and imagined a future far from the Bronx and 1210 Olmstead Avenue.

My stolen time in the front room was a lifeline, sometimes for ten minutes, other times longer. Opening the cabinet, lifting out the worn book, settling onto the couch with Aunt Jo's lamp burning next to me—all of it set the stage for a few minutes of escape from the pressure of homework and our busy home. I cried when Scarlett's magnificent home burned when soldiers took possession of her fields. My head pounded when Rhett, the handsome scoundrel, loved her for a time but left her in the end. I carried the secret of their affair tucked inside me, my blood racing when she swooned in his arms as he kissed her. I couldn't imagine such love, such passion.

I never told anyone about the book or my secret forays into the front room. They were part of my private life, one that was hard to maintain in a family of nine scrunched into a small house. Once, late at night, I heard my parents arguing from their bed on the pullout couch in the TV room. The volume on the TV was turned down; I overheard Mom say something about "money." Dad's response was too low to for me to hear. My sisters were fast asleep in their beds just inches from me. This was the first time I heard them argue about money. I finally drifted off to sleep, worried that they were mad at each other. After that, I hated to use the bathroom at night because I had to walk past my parents to get there.

SISTER DOROTHY MARIE'S ready smile and ruddy cheeks greeted me each day when I was a freshman in Saint Helena High School, an all-girls' school with the same community of Sisters who'd taught me in grammar school. Sister Dorothy Marie wasn't as beautiful as Sister Dennis Martin, but she was just as kind. Colleen was a junior in the same school and ignored me when she and her bevy of friends passed me in the halls in their matching plaid skirts and navy blazers.

My oldest brother, Francis, went to Manhattan College, a Catholic college. When he came home, he disappeared behind the door to his bedroom at the top of the stairs, an oversized closet Dad had made into a bedroom. My younger brothers were older and louder now, John, at twelve, punched Michael so often that Michael fled outside to sit on top of the mailbox on the corner. Peter, six years old, ignored all of us and curled up on his bed to read everything he could find. Mom still cleaned the kitchen floor with ammonia and retreated to her chair in the TV room. Dad returned from work so tired he'd fall asleep with his head propped up in his hands as a cigarette burned in the ashtray beside him.

When Mom's friend, Mrs. Slevin, came for a visit, I'd sit on the couch in the TV room pretending to read the newspaper so I could listen to their conversation. Mrs. Slevin and her husband were Irish and spoke with the same accent as my parents. She had gray hair, was tall and thin with a pointy chin, and she always hugged me. She gave my sisters and me $5 each to "buy something special." I was amazed when I heard Mom laugh at something Mrs. Slevin said. Mom laughed? The sound was foreign to me. The kitchen was a serious place where she spent hours cooking and cleaning. Even though I had fun with my friends, I was shocked that Mom seemed happy.

Was she different with her friends than she was with my sisters and brothers and me?

The mystery deepened when, along with Mrs. Slevin, my parents' other Irish friends—Hugh Barry and Mrs. Slevin's husband—came over to play the card game "Twenty-five" at the kitchen table.

Mr. Barry, a lumbering giant of a man with a shock of white hair and a beaming face called out, "Kathleen you're playing well tonight. Amn't I glad we're partners!"

"Go on, now, Hugh Barry." Then I heard her laugh over the shuffle of cards and the clink of ice in a glass.

I was so used to hearing the Irish words like "amn't" for "am I not" that I knew what he meant

While the group played cards that night, Dad managed to get quiet John Slevin to comment about when he played cards in Ireland. "I never thought I'd do it again after how many times I lost."

Dad laughed. "Don't worry, John. We'll send you home with some money in your pocket."

In spite of his fatigue, Dad bantered with his friends. "Dell, you're looking like a winner tonight." I imagined Mrs. Slevin blushing in response.

And to Hugh Barry, Dad said, "I hope you keep your winnings in a long and healthy life." With the slap of a card on the table Hugh Barry answered him, "It looks as though you're right, Frank." And everyone laughed. (Later I learned that Dad's comment was a lyrical way of saying "may it bring you good luck.")

As the game went on, I reimagined who my parents were—adults who needed time to relax without my brothers and sisters or me. This was when I started to grow up, to get a sense of adulthood outside my small world of school and studying and occasional time with friends. This was when I started to wonder what my life might be like when I got older.

MY PARENTS DIDN'T drink much. Dad might have a beer with dinner or a highball when he played cards. Mom liked whiskey sours made in a Waring blender. Later in life she loved Bailey's Irish Cream topped with milk. When I was fourteen, Mom's brother Jim died. I overheard my parents' whispered conversation about how he'd hit his head when he fell in the bathroom of his rooming house in Manhattan. He'd been drunk. It was the first time I realized that someone could die as a result of drinking alcohol.

When I was sixteen, I spent the summer in Massachusetts with Aunt Maggie, Dad's sister, and her husband, Jimmy. Aunt Maggie's upbeat personality was a revelation to me compared to my serious parents. Wavy red hair and rosy cheeks complemented her ready smile.

"Come over here and tell me about your day." She'd hug me before she sat me down next to her at the kitchen table. "Now, tell me—how are ye doing?"

She and Jimmy drank. Sometimes Aunt Maggie drank poteen—alcohol made from potatoes—when friends brought it back from Ireland. If she'd had a few Irish whiskeys, she'd laugh and tell stories. "Give me more of the talking drink," she'd call out to whichever of her seven children was nearby before she started in on another tale.

Uncle Jimmy, on the other hand, was not nice when he drank. "The lot of ye are good for nothin'," he'd call out from his captain's chair at the kitchen table. I'd sit on the couch in the living room reading a book, hating what came out of his mouth.

Aunt Maggie would take a long drag from her cigarette and say, "Jimmy, you don't mean any of it."

"I do. I mean all of it."

She'd get up, cook him a steak, and serve it with a baked potato and roasted carrots from the garden. One of their sons—J.J., Anthony, Sean, or Gerry—would join her in the kitchen to check on the chicken frying in the pan as their daughters—Bridie, Mary, and Margaret—came in the door.

"Ten minutes to dinner, everyone," Maggie would call out.

By the time we sat down, Jimmy would be in the living room staring at the television.

"Just ignore him, Maura," I remember Aunt Maggie saying as she filled my plate. "He's not good when he's got the drink in him."

I took a tiny bit of carrot and forced it down my throat. It was hard to ignore his brooding presence in the next room.

One night Jimmy's cousins visited from Rhode Island. Aunt Maggie, Brian's wife, and her oldest daughter, were drinking tea at the kitchen table. Jimmy and Brian stood on the front porch drinking boilermakers (beer with a shot of Irish whiskey). I watched Jimmy set the drinks on a side table before I joined the women for tea.

A few minutes later I heard Brian yell, "You ugly bastard."

Then Jimmy shouted some obscenities. When I looked out the window, I saw fists flying. The women ran over to intervene. Before they opened the screen door, Jimmy had pushed Brian over the railing. Brian screamed as he hit the driveway, ten feet below.

I stepped over to the door as Brian's wife ran out and called, "Brian, are ye all right?"

Brian got up, dusted himself off, and declared, "I'm fine. Just a bit shaken up." His wife helped him back up the stairs.

I was shocked. I'd never seen anything like it. My heart hammered in my chest as she guided him to the kitchen. I walked into the living room. I hated every minute of their drinking and nastiness. Soon after everyone got back inside, Maggie went over to Jimmy.

"You need to apologize to him, Jimmy. Now. Please."

He turned to Brian. "I got carried away. Are we good?"

Brian reached out a shaky hand. "Yes, Jimmy. We're all right. We're all right." They shook hands, laughed, and poured themselves another drink. The women returned to the table as Aunt Maggie put on the kettle for a fresh pot of tea. I'd had enough. I went into the girls' bedroom, closed the door, lay down, and stared at the ceiling.

I didn't trust Uncle Jimmy. I couldn't imagine a person as sweet as Aunt Maggie putting up with him. That summer when I returned to the Bronx, I told Mom, "I'll never marry an Irishman."

"Ah, Maura, why ever not?"

"I just won't." I kept hearing Brian's bloodcurdling scream resound in my head. I couldn't tell her what had happened. Was it loyalty? Was I ashamed of my uncle? I don't know.

Years later, when my depression escalated and I started

to drink all the time, I thought about Uncle Jimmy. Unlike him, most of the time I made sure I was alone when I drank. If I was with friends, I only had a drink or two. I didn't want any ugly scenes. But the shame I carried over my excessive drinking built up inside me until I asked for help. Using words to tell another person about my drinking was the catalyst for me to stop.

I told my truth. I wanted to live and not allow the shame of being an alcoholic hold me back.

four

THE DECISION

WHY DID ALL my years in Catholic school lead me to the convent? It was Sister Perpetua's fault. When she looked at me and said, "God loves *you*," her eyes burned through me, her face suffused with... love? My face flushed hot and I had trouble breathing. She stood there in her long white Dominican habit and black veil that was attached to that strange white headpiece so only her face showed. I'd been in Catholic school all my life and had gotten used to the way the Sisters looked. But I was sixteen and worried. I wanted to do something big with my life but I didn't know what. I wanted to go to college, but how would I pay for it? How could I study when home was filled with the constant chaos of three younger brothers?

"Mom. John punched me."

"He's lying. He pushed me first." Then John slugged Michael and ran past me laughing.

I needed a way to make a plan for myself, so I applied for scholarships and thought about becoming a nurse. My best friend, Ellen, wanted to be a nurse, so I thought I'd be one too.

In 1966 I volunteered at the Bronx Veterans' Hospital wearing a pink pinstriped pinafore bringing magazines to patients. The stench of disinfectant and urine turned my stomach as I passed male patients just a little older than me who had been wounded in the Vietnam War. The odors, the desperation finally convinced me nursing was not for me.

What about becoming a teacher? Mrs. Slevin's daughter was a teacher and she seemed happy. But, again, how could I afford college? Dad juggled three and four jobs to keep our family afloat. He and Mom were exhausted from caring for us seven kids.

Nightmares plagued me. One had me sinking knee-deep in quicksand, yelling "Help, help," before I woke up gasping for air, sheets tangled around me. I had to do something to stop the worry from crushing me.

I had no idea that Sister Perpetua, my junior year religion teacher, would change everything. She wasn't someone I confided in, or even talked to outside of class. But when she came down the aisle and skewered me with a piercing gaze and the words, "God loves YOU," she leaned in as if she knew I was searching for answers. Could she be right? For years I had repeated the mantra "God loves me." But until this moment I hadn't felt it. My heart raced. I struggled to breathe. Why hadn't I thought of it before? Maybe God *did* love me? Relief seeped in like a gentle breeze calming the anxiety that consumed me. Maybe I could be like Sister Perpetua and be a nun *and* a teacher. Aunt Jo seemed happy. So did Cousin Mary who was a teacher and a nun. But how would I know what God wanted *me* to do? There was one way to find it out.

Ask him.

Forty-five of us sat in that religion class in blue blazers, white blouses, and plaid skirts, listening, taking notes, reading the textbook. Was I the only one who heard what Sister Perpetua had said?

My best friend, Ellen, who sat next to me, raised her eyebrows at my blushing face and whispered, "What's going on?"

I shook my head.

Barbara Haberman stared at the blackboard like it held the mysteries of the universe. Anne Marie Breen rolled her eyes as Sister walked past her on the way to her desk, rosary beads clicking.

That day after school, I got off the Q44 bus across the street from our house and, instead of walking toward home, I turned left to Saint Helena Church, went up the concrete steps, opened a Naugahyde door, and tiptoed into the empty vestibule that smelled like the inside of rubber boots. I hesitated. My heart flip-flopped in my chest like it wanted to fly up to heaven. Did God know I was here? I pushed open the door to the church, dipped my fingers in the holy water font, blessed myself, and faced the altar. My heart rate slowed and my breathing eased as I slid into a pew, knelt down, and bowed my head. The aroma of beeswax and incense surrounded me before I asked, *God, should I become a nun?* I breathed in and out, in and out. I heard the clink of coins in a collection box as a woman lit a candle at the front of the church. Maybe God didn't hear me. I asked again. *God, should I become a nun?* The woman who lit the candle bent over in prayer, her black mantilla like lacy wings across her shoulders.

I repeated church visits every day after school but heard nothing from God. Hours spent poring over books in the library confirmed that the Sisters who taught me were part of the Order of Saint Dominic. And their college education had been paid for by the convent. I wouldn't need to worry about affording college. The nuns would pay. The trade-off seemed minor. I had no interest in boys, had never dated, never thought about getting married. I knew that entering the convent would be a radical thing to do, but I knew very little about what it really meant. Why not become a nun? The nuns who taught me seemed happy and were great teachers. I wanted to do something special with my life. Becoming a nun would be special, wouldn't it? If Aunt Jo and Sister Perpetua had found their way to happiness in the convent, maybe I could too.

For a long time, I didn't tell anyone about my goal to enter the convent. That included my two sisters, Colleen and Jo Anne. A year before I made the decision, when I was a sophomore, we sat in the kitchen snacking on Ritz crackers and Velveeta cheese.

"B.A. is the best," my sister Colleen said. "She cracks me up."

Jo Anne nodded. "Yeah. She's a good teacher. I need to study more."

"I'm not worried about that," Colleen said. "I'm in the commercial class, and I just need to get a job after I graduate. My friends and I kid around with B.A. She's funny."

Sunlight shone on the altar in the corner where Mom kept a red vigil light burning in front of the picture of the sacred heart of Jesus. The sun reflected off swords that pierced his heart, giving it an eerie glow. As I pulled another cracker from the box, I realized they were talking about Sister Beatrice Anthony, nicknamed B.A., the biology teacher. *She was funny?* All the Sisters who taught me were serious. Good teachers, but serious. If I became a nun, maybe I could teach biology and have fun like B.A.

Sister Dorothy Marie was my sophomore homeroom teacher and taught chemistry. She was nice, but I wouldn't call her funny. She and B.A. talked before class. The science rooms were connected, so B.A. often stopped by on her way to class.

One day soon after my sisters had talked about B.A., I heard laughter coming from inside B.A.'s classroom. I stopped what I was doing and moved closer to the doorway. Yes, there was Colleen's voice rising above the chatter. When I stole a glance into their classroom, there was B.A., eyes glinting with mischief behind rimless glasses as Colleen waved her arms while telling a story.

How did Colleen have so much fun in school? She told me about how she and her posse of friends pitched pennies on Sister Jerome's desk as the elderly nun fell asleep in Algebra class. When Sister woke up she said, "Look girls. Pennies from heaven!" From then on Colleen and her friends sang "Pennies from Heaven" as they skipped down the hall, arms slung around each other like compadres. Now I heard that refrain spilling out of B.A.'s classroom, followed by more laughter.

Two year later, in 1967, when I was a senior, my friends and I rushed down the hall to class, chatting about a physics test.

"Our study session helped a lot. I'm sure I passed." Ellen gave Jeannie a high five as the rest of us chatted about problems on the exam. As we walked by B.A.'s room, I peeked inside and remembered that she'd been friends with Colleen. I read in one of the library books that girls who wanted to enter the convent needed a Sister to sponsor them. I would have asked Sister Dorothy Marie but she had changed schools.

Maybe B.A. was an option? Even though I never had her as a teacher, maybe her friendship with Colleen could help me. Since everything about my quest to become a nun was serious—from praying in church to reading books about religious life—maybe B.A. could bring some fun into the equation. I'd kept my decision to enter the convent to myself. It was something special, something just for me, not something to be talked about with family or classmates. I'd decided to keep it to myself as long as possible so I could savor it in private. But I needed to talk with a Sister who'd sponsor me.

When I got up the nerve to talk to her, a new gaggle of girls was busy cleaning blackboards and microscopes. Chalk dust filled the air as a student ran an eraser in wide circles through chalk diagrams of protozoa and spirochetes on the blackboard. The aroma of alcohol wafted toward me as another student cleaned microscopes. When I stepped inside the room it hit me—*what if B.A. said no?* Her petite frame was bent over a black-topped lab table as she sorted assignments. The Dominican habit and black veil that enveloped her five-foot height did little to dampen the spirit of the song she was humming. Was it "If I Had a Hammer?"

She'd just gotten to the line ". . . it's the bell of freedom . . ." when she looked up and smiled. "Hello. Can I help you?"

"Hi, Sister. I'm Maura Doherty, Colleen's sister."

She smiled. "How is Colleen? I miss her. She and her friends were a lot of fun."

I took a breath. "She's working downtown at an insurance company and likes it." I didn't know much about Colleen's job. She left every morning, her dark blue skirt and jacket newly pressed, black heels gleaming with polish. She told me how to pronounce her company's name.

"It's spelled MONY, Maura, but it sounds like money. They make money."

I hoped Sister didn't notice me rubbing my sweaty palms on my skirt as I spoke. She, on the other hand, looked cool and composed in layers of white and black.

Her smile widened. "Tell her I said hi."

I took a shaky breath. "Sister, I have something I want to talk to you about."

She must have noticed the tension in my voice and called to her helpers. "Thanks, everyone. That will be all for today."

The girls stopped their chores, said goodbye, and left.

"Why don't we sit?" She pulled stools over to the table and we sat down.

I swallowed, then blurted out, "Sister, I want to enter the convent."

Her eyes opened wider as my stomach tightened.

"Oh? Tell me more." There was a softness to her despite the plastic band that rimmed her forehead and held up her veil. A white headpiece hid all traces of hair, but her eyes sparked with curiosity.

"I've been praying about it a lot. About being a nun like you, living in the convent with the other Sisters and teaching science. It's what I want to do after I graduate."

She lowered her gaze and pulled the edges of her scapula taut before she looked at me. "Okay. Why don't we make a plan to meet after school and talk some more? Does that sound alright with you?"

I nodded. "Sounds good, Sister. I'd like that." My shoulders relaxed as the anxiety I'd been carrying came down a notch. I had told a Sister my secret and I was glad.

I BECAME ONE of B.A.'s helpers, cleaning equipment and chalk boards. After the other students left, we'd talk. I told her about my forays into church to pray for guidance, how I admired the Sisters, how I wanted to be like them. Like her.

She told me, "I entered with a group of young women. We teach school and love it." With that her smile stretched into a grin that lit up her face and she laughed like she did with Colleen. The more time I spent with her the more I felt like I was making the right decision. Even the constant tumult caused by my younger brothers annoyed me less. My nightmares stopped. I had a plan.

Early that spring B.A. asked, "Have you told your parents?"

My throat seized. "Not yet." They'd supported me when I volunteered at the Veterans' Hospital. Mom had ironed the pinstripe pinafore before each shift and Dad had given me rides when he could. And they understood when I'd decided not to become a nurse.

When I told them, "I'll become a teacher, like Mrs. Slevin's daughter, Elizabeth," they'd nodded.

Now B.A. told me, "Maura, if you want to enter, you will need your parents' permission to visit the motherhouse with me. You'll need a note from them saying it's okay."

I swallowed hard. *My parents will be surprised, but I'm sure they'll support me. Won't they?* Until then I'd kept my decision to myself, savoring the secret that God had given me a vocation. As I wrote down what the note needed to say, my hand trembled and the letters slid into each other. I felt as if I was asking to go on a field trip to Rockland County with my favorite nun. Only this would be no ordinary field trip.

I'd see something few others did—the inside of the motherhouse, where girls became nuns.

Our high school had a tradition where seniors guessed who from their class might enter the convent. Every year one or two did. Ellen asked, "Maura, who do you think will enter? Maybe Cathy or Jan or even Barbara? They seem like they could be the ones."

My face flushed as I lowered my eyes to the trigonometry book. "I have no idea, Ellen. Let's finish this, then go over our French homework."

I hated lying to her. She'd never guess it could be me. Yes, I was a good student, but become a nun? No way. Ellen knew nothing about my conversations with B.A. or my frequent visits to church.

She sighed, opened the book, and read over the next problem.

I'd tell her soon, but first I had to tell my parents.

✧

THE SMELL OF turpentine and enamel paint wafted over me as I mounted the stairs where Dad was painting the upstairs hall. My stomach gurgled as I got closer. This was my chance to talk to him without my siblings listening in. My sweaty palm gripped the handrail until I got to the top step. He stood on a ladder, moving the brush up and down the wall like a maestro conducting in slow tempo, pausing to dip the brush into a can of dark green paint. He'd fashioned a paper bag, its edges turned up, into a painter's hat. If I wasn't so nervous, I would have laughed at how he looked. But this was serious.

Dad looked down. "Hello, Maura. How are you?" He held the brush over the paint tray as he looked at me.

"I'm good Dad. But I need to talk with you." I swallowed hard, my head pounding.

"Oh, do you now? Let me finish this bit and I'll be right down." He cut the last of the paint into the corner, lay down the brush, came down the ladder, and sat next to me on the top step. "Well, what is it now?"

He smelled of solvents and sweat. *What should I say? What would he say?* My heart beat so fast I felt faint, so I put my hands on either side of me, the nubby brown carpet my anchor.

"Dad." The bags under his eyes showed fatigue. I wanted to throw my arms around him and comfort him, not turn his world upside down. I took a breath. "I've decided to enter the convent."

He stared at me and, for a moment, I couldn't breathe. Flecks of paint on his paper-bag hat matched the ones on his work shirt. Green for hope, for new life.

Then his eyes filled with tears. "Ah, Maura," he choked out. This father of mine who barely had time for anything but work. Who loved to chat with our neighbor Tommy Donlon as he walked home from the subway. Who'd do anything for Aunt Jo, the cloistered nun, and Cousin Mary, the Sister of Charity. This father of mine splotched with paint leaned toward me, his face crumpled with concern.

"Why don't you go to college first? Then, if you still want to enter the convent, I'll help you."

I sagged, saved only by my hands on the ugly carpet. I forced myself to sit up straight, like he wanted when he said, "Touch the line." Which meant I had to sit up straight like I had a book on my head and needed to keep it steady. Today I needed to keep myself steady,

"No, Dad. The convent will pay for college so I can be a teacher and a nun. I start classes in September at Saint Thomas Aquinas College which is run by the Sisters. I enter the convent in August."

With this he bowed his head, cupped his chin in his paint-streaked hands anointed with the color of his Irish homeland, and cried. This father of mine whom I'd never seen cry, cried. I leaned into him and put my arm around his shoulder as his paper bag hat slid to one side of his head. My heart sank. I had thought he'd be happy for me, relieved that I'd be taken care of. I reminded myself what was at stake—my future as a teaching nun.

After a few minutes, he asked, "Have you told your mother?"

"Not yet."

We sat there, thinking our thoughts, me of the long white habit, black veil, and rosary beads. And him? Perhaps he thought of his middle daughter who, in a few months, would leave home to enter a place of mystery and godliness.

I left him there, staring into space, tears on his face.

Mom was in the kitchen stirring a pot on the stove, spoon in one hand, cigarette in the other. When I told her my plan, she said, "Oh, Maura," and stared at the gravy as if it held a secret. After a minute she looked at me. "Have you told your father?"

"Yes."

She nodded, took another puff, smoke mixing with the steam rising above the stove.

I'd never talked with my parents about nuns or God or

the Catholic church. My becoming a nun wasn't something any of us expected. I thought this was what God wanted for me. What *I* wanted for me. He had chosen me to become a nun dedicated to helping others—with the added bonus of a free college education.

part two

During

CELTIC CROSS

five

NOVITIATE

1967–1976

I WALKED UP the beige concrete steps of my new home in the novitiate at the Dominican Sisters' motherhouse in Sparkill, New York, black suitcase in hand. The front door pulled me like a magnet, offering to give me the life I'd been praying for.

Finally. I'm here.

Sunlight glared off my glasses as Dad called out, "Maura." I paused, turned around, and waved as he held up an instamatic camera. Was I saying goodbye to the old me or hello to my new life? Mom, my six siblings, Aunt Maggie, Ellen, and other friends and family stood nearby. Mom clutched her leather purse, her hair pulled around a black hat, its matching veil cinched with bobby pins. Her gray hair was curled and had a tint of blue thanks to her visit to the Shear Charm salon.

Decades earlier my parents had seen Aunt Jo and Cousin Mary enter the convent. Had Dad taken photos of them too?

Everyone waved. Ellen's tears streamed down her cheeks. Fear bubbled up inside me. When would I see her again? When would I see my family again? I swallowed hard, turned, and walked up the remaining steps. My hand trembled as I reached to open the door. *Am I doing the right thing? Is this what I really want?* I took a breath and stepped inside.

Over two dozen young girls were scattered across the room. Black tights and white undershirts spilled out of their suitcases while they took off dresses, skirts, and blouses. Sisters hovered over them like mother hens, exchanging each brightly colored outfit for a black one. Where was my sponsor? I spotted B.A. in the opposite corner and picked my way around several nuns who nodded as I passed. My heart thudded so hard I almost lost my balance but forced myself to keep walking.

I'm here. I'm ready.

"Welcome, Maura. How are you?" B.A.'s smile puffed up her pink cheeks.

"I'm okay." My lungs squeezed out another breath.

She reached over to hug me. I leaned in but felt wooden, as if my joints had solidified. She released me, nodded to a chair that was upholstered in a design of yellow roses—yellow, like the ones we grew at home, the peace rose Dad had brought home from the World's Fair in Queens. Tears choked me. *When will I see our roses again?*

She pointed to black fabric spread across the arm of the chair. "Your postulant outfit is ready."

When I put the suitcase down, my hand tingled from the tight grip that had carried it from the car.

"Here's what you'll be wearing." She leaned over and picked up something long and bulky, holding it against me like a prom dress, except that it was black and came to the middle of my calves. "It looks like it will fit. The cape goes over it." She held out something that looked like a ballerina skirt fit for a dirge.

"Okay." All that praying and I never thought, what do

new nuns wear? I knew about their work as teachers but not much else. I never asked B.A. about my new outfit or what life would be like after I entered. What had I gotten myself into?

She gestured to the suitcase at my feet. "Do you have your slip and panty hose?"

I nodded, knelt down, unzipped the case, and pulled out a white slip and black panty hose. "Do I need an undershirt too?"

"Yes. I almost forgot that."

We locked eyes for a minute before I began to undress in this room filled with dozens of other girls doing the same thing. My fingers fumbled with buttons until the jacket slid off. I turned so B.A. could pull down the zipper on the matching dress. It was my favorite, beige and brown plaid with red accents, bought on sale at Alexander's department store on Fordham Road. Slashes of red caught my eye as I pulled the dress over my head. *No more red. No more plaid. No more bolero jackets.* I offered this up to Our Lady. *Sweet Mother of God, you didn't know what you were getting into either, did you? Help me do the right thing.* I folded every item and put them on the chair, covering the roses with what I used to wear. I exchanged my slip with a lace border for a cotton half-slip with an elastic waist. Off came the bra before I pulled on a white T-shirt just like the one Dad wore every day, the kind Mom hated because they got so dirty. As I smoothed the wrinkles of the new T-shirt I wondered, *How is Dad doing? Will he cry when he sees me dressed as a nun?* I took a deep breath, sat down, peeled off beige panty hose, and replaced them with a thick black pair. "What's next, Sister?"

She unsnapped the front of the new dress before I stepped into it. It was like stepping into another world, this one heavy and awkward, as if I'd been draped in a thick bedspread. So different from the soft cotton dress I'd taken off.

God, I do this for you.

As B.A. snapped the dress closed, I looked over the room. Every surface was covered in clothing as young girls struggled with dark hose, elastic banded slips, and heavy dresses with snaps. I put on a leather belt and tightened it around my waist before B.A. draped a short, black cape around my shoulders. "Now these." She held out two white cuffs with plastic edges that dug into my wrists after I slid them on. She tied a matching collar with a black ribbon around my neck to complete the outfit. I was encased in black cloth and white plastic, nothing like anything I'd ever worn before. Uncomfortable as I was, I knew this was the price I needed to pay to become a full-fledged nun.

"Rosary beads?

"Yes, from my Aunt Jo, blessed by the Pope."

B.A.'s eyes softened as she draped the slender black beads over the belt. "Shoes?"

I bent over the suitcase, awkward in the new outfit, unused to the belted waist and cumbersome dress and cape. I sat on the edge of the chair gazing at the rose pattern, an oasis in the tumult around me. Then I leaned over, put one shoe on, did the same with the second one, and tied the laces in a double knot. When I'd brought them home from the store on Delancey Street, Colleen called them "old lady shoes." They laced across the front up to the ankle. I thought about how Cousin Mary had taken me shopping for these shoes. The store had smelled musty as if fresh air had never touched the long rows of black mantles, sturdy leather shoes, and other Sisterly gear. The convent had sent me a list of things to bring and provided the address of specific stores that catered to nuns. The list included: two pair of sturdy black leather shoes, one pair for everyday wear and another for special occasions; two white cotton half-slips; five white short-sleeve undershirts; cotton pajamas in solid colors (white, blue, or gray [no red]); nonskid slippers; a twin-size corded bedspread in black, blue, gray, or brown.

"Mom," I said, when I read over the list, "What's a corded bedspread?"

"It's a kind of cotton. I'll buy you one at Alexander's."

Now, with the new laced-up shoes on my feet, I felt awkward. Like I needed to learn how to walk all over again, weighed down by the heavy garments assigned to the new nuns.

When I looked up, I noticed several girls were walking toward the front door, all of them in black.

"One more thing," B.A. said as she held up a short black veil rimmed in white plastic.

Something inside me said, *It's not too late. Don't put on the veil.* I looked at B.A., the Sister who had guided me to this moment and supported me when I'd poured out my secret longing to become a nun. I took a long breath, stood up, and bent my head so she could position the veil on my head. Chills ran down me as she tied it behind my neck.

When I looked up, I realized what was missing—a mirror. There were no mirrors. I had no idea how I looked. Even our modest home on Olmstead Avenue had mirrors.

She straightened my veil, and using a finger, she tucked my hair in and asked, "Ready?"

"Ready." I walked out the door in my new outfit to join my family and friends before the blessing ceremony at the Saint Agnes chapel. Dad took photos and Mom dabbed her eyes when they saw me. We all hugged then walked around the pond outside the motherhouse. I felt awkward and stumbled slightly in the new shoes. I was off balance for a good reason. I had grabbed one shoe with a low heel and another with a higher heel from identical boxes. I tilted to one side. When a friend pointed it out, I went back inside and changed one of the shoes.

And now I felt new, eager to begin my new life as Sister Kathleen Maura. After we walked around the pond that surrounded the statue of the Blessed Virgin Mary, I hugged my family and friends goodbye and joined the rest of the postulants. Sister Margaret Gerard led us to the front choir stalls that faced the side of the chapel. I could see my parents, who were sitting a few rows back. Mom was bent over her rosary beads and Dad smiled at me. I smiled back then looked at the priest who had his back to us as he read a prayer in Latin. I swallowed the lump that formed in my throat.

This was my choice. It was time to leave my family behind and start my new life.

✧

IN 1967, TWENTY-EIGHT of us entered the convent of the Dominican Sisters of Our Lady of the Rosary in Sparkill, just an hour from my home in the Bronx. In spite of the differences in my previous life, some things were familiar, especially the crucifixes in every room. A life-sized one hung in the chapel, much larger than the one in the church back home. Lots of other things about the convent were unexpected, including the terminology. I was Catholic, had studied vocabulary and even took Latin in high school, but I was unfamiliar with the new words coming at me. During one of her first talks, Sister Margaret Gerard stood in front of us in the study hall.

"I am the Postulant Mistress. You ask me and only me if you have questions."

Now I had a mistress?

"Sisters, the group sitting here, the ones you entered with, are called a band. You have started your first year as postulants in the Dominican Congregation of Our Lady of the Rosary."

Funny, I thought, a band with no musical instruments. I knew about Our Lady and had prayed the rosary many times, but "the band" was a new one on me.

"In two weeks you will start classes at Saint Thomas Aquinas College located down the path from the motherhouse. All but one of you will be pre-registered as freshman with a full academic course load. Sister Kathleen Mary, you already have your college degree. Please talk with me after this meeting about your responsibility at the college. The rest of you will receive your class schedules next week."

She continued, "We are called Sisters, not nuns. Nuns are Sisters who live in cloisters. Dominican Sisters are a teaching order who follow in the footsteps of Saint Dominic."

Aunt Jo was a cloistered nun even though we were both Sisters. This was confusing.

And "postulant." I didn't blink when Sister Margaret Gerard said this. I stared straight ahead with the rest of the group. Postulant sounded nasty—like a pus-filled thing with a lance through it. The definition was nicer—"one who petitions or is a candidate." I was a candidate, petitioning to become a Sister. Then she said, "Do not attempt to speak to the novices—the Sisters with white veils—who live on the floor above ours. They are in the second year of novitiate, a year of meditation and prayer before they take final vows. Postulants and novices are in the process of formation. You are being formed into religious Sisters."

I need to be formed? I barely knew who I was, but now they would form me into a Sister? I swallowed hard and made up my mind. *If that's what's needed, I'm ready.*

She added that we could talk with novices and professed Sisters on certain feast days when we were granted "fusion," a time to speak with the Sisters who were usually off limits.

I'd seen the novices in the halls, robed in white from head to toe, gliding to and from the chapel like albino spaceships—eyes downcast, hands tucked beneath white scapulars. I knew that the word novice meant new. Sister Margaret Gerard's eyes shone as she said this, as if she were saying, "They're special, don't even try to approach them." But I had insider information. Even the ethereal habit couldn't hide the ungainly stride of Marion Farrell, the former varsity basketball player from my high school who had entered the convent the year before me. She looked up and smiled as we passed in the hall. Yes, it was definitely Marion.

And vows. The handbook I'd read explained that, after the novice year, Sisters took final vows of poverty, chastity, and obedience. *Final. Vows. Like, that's it. Over. Done.* That seemed a long way off as I strained to understand what Sister Margaret Gerard was saying now.

None of us in that room had any idea that a freight train called Vatican II was headed toward us, ready to change everything. We had no clue that the novices who had entered the year before us would be the last group to take final vows after their two-year novitiate.

"We are the 'Dominican Congregation of Our Lady of

the Rosary,'" the Postulant Mistress continued. "We are a community of Sisters who follow the teachings of Saint Dominic. He was a renowned preacher and teacher. Many of you will become Sisters who teach in Catholic schools throughout New York and Saint Louis. We also have Sisters caring for the needy in Pakistan."

I focused on what mattered most to me. *Yes. I want to be a Sister teaching high school science.*

"Novitiate" was another strange word. Postulants were the lowest ranking members of the novitiate housed within the motherhouse. I blinked at the word motherhouse. I had a mother named Kathleen. But I was told that the novitiate was part of the motherhouse. I guessed it had to do with the Mother Superior living here, in this case, Mother Marie Evangelista. The nameplate on her office door in the front hall of the motherhouse read "Mother General." Was I in her army? She lived in the farthest wing of the motherhouse with Mother Kevin, the former Mother Superior.

All of this was new—the outfit, the language, the focus on God in everything—all of it transported me into a different world where I had no compass, no way of knowing where I was headed. I had to trust that I was on the right path.

Soon after I entered the convent, I got to know Mother Kevin when I drove her to her doctor's appointment. I have Mary Mooney to thank for me getting my driver's license. Mary Mooney, Sister John Carmel, was a friend of Mom's who had entered the same convent as I had and came to visit several months before I entered. Her advice, "Get your driver's license before you enter. You'll have more freedom."

I did just that. I never questioned why she said this as she sipped tea at our kitchen table. Her matter-of-fact attitude was enough. Freedom. Who didn't want that? On second thought, I wasn't sure I did. I was entering a convent, after all. My goal was to go to college to become a teaching Sister. But I knew I should listen to someone who'd already taken final vows. I told my father, the driver in our family, that I wanted to learn how to drive. No worries. How hard could it be?

We lived in the Bronx, a borough clogged with cars and trucks, many double-parked, thanks to alternate-side-of-the-street parking requirements. Several days a week, New York City required its citizens to rotate the side of the street where they parked to allow a sweeper to wash the street. My father had a car with a stick shift, so he asked his friend, Mr. Nolan, to teach me. Mr. Nolan's car was an automatic—much easier to drive.

Mr. Nolan was a patient man. Luckily, I caught on quickly because I only had a few months to get my license before I left for the convent. When the man from the Department of Motor Vehicles got into the car with me for the road test, I was ready, even when he asked me to parallel park with a flat tire sitting in the spot he pointed to. He must not have wanted me to do well because he frowned when I managed to park without hitting the tire. I passed. I thought that getting my driver's license was God's way of saying I was definitely on the right path.

In 1967, I was a postulant, all of eighteen, living in the motherhouse in Rockland County, New York, and had declared myself a licensed driver on my convent application. And what did the former Mother Superior Mother Kevin do? She asked the Postulant Mistress to assign a lowly postulant with a driver's license to drive her to her appointments. And, of course, when asked, I said yes.

Why would a former Mother Superior ask an eighteen-year-old postulant to drive her without asking if she had any driving experience? That's what happened. And did I inform her I had just gotten my license the month before I entered? No, I did not. And where did Mother Kevin need to go? Manhattan. Had I ever driven in Manhattan? Of course not. *Dad* had driven me there. But did I tell Mother Kevin that? No.

1967. No GPS or Siri. I navigated a boat-sized black Lincoln Town Car from Rockland County to Manhattan with Mother Kevin and her companion in the back seat. The car was a luxury sedan, twice as big as Mr. Nolan's. I almost hyperventilated as I backed out of the garage. *Do not crash. Do not crash*, I repeated over and over to myself. Several miles later when my knees finally stopped shaking, I realized that the car drove like a dream, 25 miles down Route 134 onto the Palisades Parkway, over the Tappan Zee Bridge and Sprain Brook Parkway to the West Side Highway and the East Side of Manhattan for Mother Kevin's doctor's appointment on Park Avenue. Yes, Park Avenue. I'm sure she directed me from the back seat, but I don't remember.

By the time I pulled in front of the building and a doorman opened the rear passenger door, I stopped gripping the steering wheel like a life preserver. While I waited for the two Sisters, I fingered my rosary beads. When the appointment was finished, Mother Kevin and her companion got back in the car.

"Sister Kathleen Maura, I need to stop in Queens before we return to the motherhouse."

Queens? I had an aunt who lived in Queens. Would that help me get there? Mother Kevin directed me on to the 59th Street Bridge. What could go wrong if God was on my side? Then it started to rain. Not a downpour, but enough that I needed to turn on the windshield wipers. I probed the dashboard for the switch for the wipers and on they went. Problem solved.

But then I started to hum. "Slow down, you move too fast. You got to make the morning last..."

I was so captivated with driving over the very bridge that Simon and Garfunkel sang about that I didn't see that the car in front of me had stopped.

Until I rear-ended it.

"Oh, Sister, what in heaven's name has happened?" called Mother Kevin from the back seat after we crashed.

I was too scared to answer. My cheeks flamed hot as my hands strangled the steering wheel. *I crashed. I crashed. Oh, my God, I crashed the car with Mother Kevin in it.* And if this wasn't enough, I watched in horror as the driver of the car I'd hit got out of his car and marched toward us, his fists clenched, ready to do battle. I rolled down the window with a shaky hand. He looked in, glared at me, then at the back seat, and said, "Uhhh. Sorry, Sister," and strode back to his car, more than likely cursing the Sisters from his Catholic school days.

We made it back to the motherhouse while I prayed, *Please don't let them send me home.*

Mother Kevin stopped me in the hallway a week later and asked if I was aware there had been extensive damage to the front end of the car.

"No," I told her, "I didn't know."

And I didn't. I had gotten out of that car, rushed to my room, closed the door, never looked back, and hoped she never asked me to drive her again.

She didn't.

⟡

CLOSING THE DOOR to my own room was a new experience, something I'd never had at home. My convent bed was a twin, larger than my high-riser back in Olmstead Avenue. The novitiate was quiet. No television blaring, no rumble of traffic from the Cross Bronx Expressway. Back home I'd learned to tune out the horns and screech of brakes as vehicles careened into each other on the highway near our home.

I can't recall if the quiet of the novitiate scared me. I remember my stomach being tied in knots, as I worried they'd realize how unworthy I was. I missed calling Ellen to see how nursing school was, and to ask if her mother still called her a "horse's ass." I loved escaping the routine of the novitiate when I shut the door to my room where no one could see me, where I could lie down and just breathe. The door didn't lock but that didn't bother me. The room was mine, its starkness a comfort—the navy blue bedspread, a sink, a dark blue towel with *Sister Kathleen Maura* written on the label in indelible pen, the crucifix over the bed, the narrow desk and hardback chair, the small bookcase set into the headboard.

All of it, mine.

When I closed the door to my room, only God knew what I did behind that door.

And what did I do? Not much. Sometimes I read from spiritual books. But mostly I finished assignments from my classes, then lay on my bed and did absolutely nothing, waiting for the next chore, the next class I'd be taking at the college, the next meal that would need serving. During those rare moments, I just lay on that bed, soaking in the quiet, as my breathing eased.

SISTER MARY DOREEN did not like to sit still. Even when it was her turn to clean the floor, she'd prop a book on the top of the wooden handle of the dust mop and walk down the hall, eyes glued to the book, freeing a hand now and then to turn the page. She told me she'd never cleaned anything in her life and didn't want to learn now. That was our main job, cleaning the novitiate—the common areas like the community room and refectory, and the hall that led to the Mother General's office. And Sister Mary Doreen always had a book with her, immersed in Teilhard de Chardin or Descartes as the mop slid over pristine floors.

Me? I scrubbed toilets and sinks and wet-mopped bathrooms and shower rooms like my life depended on it. And it did. I'd be judged on how well I cleaned, how I did in my college classes, how prayerful I appeared as I walked down the hall. I scoured immaculate toilets, concentrating on each stroke to wash away invisible stains. Since the novitiate building was only a year old, nothing was dirty. And no dust had a chance with the cadre of postulant cleaners.

During that first year, several postulants left. They just disappeared, their rooms empty. We never heard why. I stayed and followed the rules. I didn't talk to professed Sisters, the ones with the black veils, or the novices with the white veils. I only talked to Sisters in my band when absolutely necessary and then, only in whispers. We were told we could talk in our college classes but that was it. Other than that, no radio or television, no newspapers or magazines. It was 1967.

Think Vietnam War, peace rallies, rock and roll, and hippies. I missed it all—for God, for a higher good, for the goal of gaining the white habit, black veil, and long rosary beads. I focused on what was right in front of me and I did everything I was told.

What I gained: chanting in Latin several times a day starting at 6:00 a.m.—postulants, novices, professed Sisters, raising our voices together to God; Lauds first; then Mass, the Angelus at noon; Vespers at 5:00 p.m., Compline after that. Praying all the time. Knowing that all of us prayed all the time. Even when I cleaned toilets or dust-mopped marble floors, I was part of something bigger. I prayed and stayed away from the Sisters who broke the rules, who talked to each other after we went to bed. The hours between 10:00 p.m. and 6:00 a.m. were called the Grand Silence when we were supposed to be praying and sleeping. Looking back, I know that the Sisters who broke the rules were forming friendships and letting off steam that built up under the restrictions of novitiate life. Me? I shut down and prayed.

> *Exaudi Domine, ad mea verba, intelligere meam et clamor meus.*
>
> *Hearten ad vocem orationem meam Domine meus, rex, et Deus meus.*
>
> *Give ear, O Lord, to my words, understand my cry.*
> *Hearken to the voice of my prayer, O my King and my God.*

◆

BEING SISTER KATHLEEN Maura took all my energy. Every ounce of my eighteen-year-old self was focused on succeeding in this new life. When my head hit the pillow, I slept. When Sister Margaret Gerard rang the bell at 5:00 a.m., I dragged myself out of bed, went down the hall to the communal bathroom, and walked back to my room, head lowered, praying for guidance.

Oh, Lord, help me to become holy, to do your will today.

We lined up to walk to the chapel, our breath frosty on cold mornings, to chant Lauds in Latin in a chapel not much warmer than outside. We sat across from the novices dressed in white and the professed Sisters in black veils in the surrounding pews. As the last note bounced off the chapel walls, we meditated. Most of the time I fell asleep until it was time for Mass, then rushed back to serve breakfast, something I knew how to do. But as for the rest of it—meditating, the being holy all the time—I had no clue. I was in a panic, palms sweating as I clenched my hands under the short black cape, terrified they would find out I didn't know what I was doing.

I watched the other Sisters, especially the novices. Even though I couldn't talk with them, I knew a few from high school. Sister Grace was a flaming redhead who towered over everyone. Somehow the long white habit made her look taller. And now that gorgeous hair was covered in a skull cap and long white veil. The only red that showed was her eyebrows.

She left notes in my prayer book to encourage me. All the novices did this for the postulants. The notes were called, "dinghies," and they included holy cards drawn in India ink with messages like "I'm praying for you." Grace stared at me from across the chapel where our choir stalls faced each other, her eyebrows telegraphing her concern. They shot up if I looked tired, and they relaxed if I looked at ease—a kind of Morse code for the novitiate.

Now I know it made no sense that we didn't talk with the ones who knew the most about being Sisters since they'd been at it longer. I accepted everything they told me, prayed, put my head down, and did what I was told. When I was assigned to serve breakfast, I lowered my head and slipped serving bowls on the table without a word. I knew some of the Sisters from having attended twelve years in their schools. Almost all of them respected the rule not to talk to postulants.

But some of them didn't—namely, Sister Redempta.

Sister Redempta had been my fourth-grade teacher, striding down the classroom aisle, tall and lean. She loved Canada Mints, a fluorescent pink candy that dissolved in the mouth with minty sweetness. My father bought them for her, and, when I handed them to her, her eyes widened with the joy we candy lovers share.

When I was in eighth grade, I'd helped her class. She seemed much older by then, a gaunt frame who walked up and down the aisles with a voice that crackled, "No talking. Write 'talking' on your paper if you are talking."

Some students did what she asked. They wrote 'talking' on their paper because Sister always knew who was talking, so why not admit it?

I noticed something else, too. Every so often she'd step into the walk-in closet at the back of the room and close the door. I wondered what she was doing there in the dark. A few times I caught a glimpse of her drinking from a thermos, the kind my father used for coffee. Within a few minutes, she'd re-emerge, her cheeks glowing as she repeated, "Write 'talking' on your paper if you are talking." I never found out what was in that thermos.

By the time I entered the novitiate, Sister Redempta had retired and was living in the infirmary on the top floor of the motherhouse. She was almost skeletal, eyes sunken into her skull, cheekbones protruding through translucent skin, shuffling down the hall like she'd lost her way. The skull cap that held her veil and bandeau puckered around her face. But she remembered me and called out, "Maura," in a voice that echoed through the hall. Like an obedient postulant, I lowered my head and walked away.

One day as I wiped down refectory tables, she said, "Maura, I'm hungry. Please get me food."

I kept working. *I'm not Maura anymore, I'm Sister Kathleen Maura.* I remembered the candy I'd brought her in school. But that was years ago. Now I was a first-year postulant, worried that someone would overhear her and, suspecting I'd been talking, would report me. I didn't want to get in trouble. The kitchen was locked. I wanted to do was finish my job, go to my room, and close the door.

"Maura, please."

I whispered, "Sister Redempta, I'm sorry. I have no way to get you food."

Her brown eyes bulged as she yelled, "An apple, a banana, anything. Maura, you must help me."

"Sister Redempta, I can't help you."

Rheumy eyes stared back at me, perhaps as she remembered the kindness of Canada Mints in a previous life.

"It's not the banana, Maura. It's the principle of the banana." With that she raised her hands, the wide sleeves of her habit revealing skinny arms that flapped up and down as she walked away, crying, "No. Oh, no."

My body sagged as I watched her leave. How could I have let her down? There I was, trying to be silent like her former students who'd followed the rules. And there was Sister Redempta, asking for my help, hungry for food, for a connection with someone from her past. As I look back, I realize she craved nourishment and compassion, things I'd put aside so I could become someone else's idea of what good was. I had no idea if she had missed a meal or didn't want to eat with the other Sisters. All I knew was I didn't help her.

It took more than a decade for me to find my way back to my connection to myself and to the "principle of the banana."

⋄

MY FATHER FOUND a way to see me more than once a month when families were allowed to visit. Soon after I entered, he said, "I wonder if the Sisters need volunteers to help? This is a pretty big place. I bet they could use some help."

I said, "No. They don't." If he volunteered it might look like I got special treatment. Other Sisters only saw their family once a month. Little did I know that even I, his rule-abiding daughter, couldn't stop Dad from asking if he could help out—just so he could see me for a few extra minutes.

I found out that he'd followed through with his plan one Saturday when he showed up with shovels and a wheelbarrow to plant a garden on the novitiate patio, an area filled with waist-high thistles and out-of-control weeds. I worried about him and the work it would require. Then, I worried about me. What would my fellow postulants think? I prayed to be humble, to not let his good deeds conflict with my need to be good, to not stand out from the other Sisters.

He continued this for weeks and soon produced a miracle of chrysanthemums and evergreens, flowers of all kinds, and bulbs planted for spring. In spite of my worries, I loved seeing him for five minutes when he finished for the day. I doubt my fellow Sisters were anything but grateful. His hard work added beauty to our lives, ones dedicated to prayer, meditation, cleaning bathrooms and spotless floors, and taking classes at the college run by the Sisters.

On his last day in the garden, I helped put his tools in the trunk of the car.

"Dad, you're the best."

"Now, Maura, I love to help. In fact, Sister Margaret Gerard and I have been talking. It seems she's willing to take me up on my offer to drive all of you down to see the Christmas lights at Rockefeller Center. I volunteered to drive the bus."

I stared at him. "But, Dad, you don't know how to drive a bus."

"Maura, at the moment I may not know how to drive a bus, but Tommy Donlon knows how to drive a big truck. That's close enough. He'll teach me. By the time the holidays come, I'll be right as rain. Plus, with you and all the Sisters praying for me, what could go wrong?"

Plenty, I thought, and watched his car pull away from the novitiate. I was terrified. Dad was generous and thought little of himself. Our neighbor, Tommy Donlon, with his tribe of ten children, might be his friend, but he wouldn't be there to help Dad if he got into trouble. But what did I know? I was just a postulant.

I told my friend, Sister Mary Doreen, "I'm afraid that we'll have an accident and my father will be responsible."

"Oh, Maura," she said as she rolled her eyes. "He'll do fine. He wouldn't offer if he couldn't do it." She was from Manhattan and was eager for a trip downtown, even if it was in a bus packed with postulants, novices, and an amateur bus driver.

The motherhouse rented a yellow school bus. I sat behind Dad, praying we wouldn't drive over the edge of the Palisades Parkway into the Hudson River as I slid my rosary beads between my sweaty fingers. *Please let us be okay, dear Lord. Don't let us crash.*

Mary Doreen sat next to me, her eyes glued to the Manhattan skyline as we drove over the George Washington Bridge. "Maura, look."

But I didn't look. I stared straight ahead, over my father's shoulder, as he navigated past a tanker truck and a Greyhound bus filled with passengers.

Please, Lord.

We took the exit for the West Side Highway along the Hudson River into Midtown Manhattan.

God, keep us in your sight.

The babble of voices around me turned quiet as we took the 42nd Street ramp past Times Square and headed uptown. Dad put on the hazard lights and pulled in front of the skating rink at Rockefeller Center. The bus filled with oohs and ahhs from awestruck Sisters, many of whom had never been to Manhattan, no less seen its renowned Christmas tree. Even though I'd seen it before, the view from the bus seemed even more magnificent.

"Well, now. Here we are," said Dad as he turned off the engine and pulled the emergency brake.

Sister Margaret Gerard had made it clear that, because we were postulants and novices, protected from the outside world, we couldn't get off the bus. Instead, we crowded the windows and stared at the tree, ablaze with lights as it towered over dozens of ice skaters on the rink below. I loved the magic before me and was glad Dad had gotten us there to see it. I slipped the rosary beads back onto my belt.

When Sister Margaret Gerard gave the word, we got back in our seats, Dad started the bus, and I grabbed my rosaries again.

God, thank you for getting us here. Now all you have to do is get us back to the motherhouse.

※

WHEN I BECAME a postulant, the statues seemed bigger than the ones I'd seen in my parish church. Maybe because there were so many of them. The ones in the chapel were life-sized. Mary's altar was the most popular. Sisters knelt in front of it all the time and lit candles that carried the aroma of beeswax to me in the front choir stall. There was even a statue of her in the pond outside the chapel.

And Jesus. The crucifix over the altar was huge, much bigger than the one in our church back home. Jesus looked miserable since someone had pounded nails through his hands and feet, so he hung there in agony. But I didn't think about that. The cross was a sign of hope that he would rise from the dead and that I'd go to heaven if I was good.

I was very good. During my first year in novitiate, I did what Sister Margaret Gerard said. She never yelled. She talked quietly and looked sincere. I would do anything to please her—I even set my clock a half hour early to be the first in line to go to chapel.

The next year I became a novice.

I have no memory of the actual day of the event. The only reminder is a photo of me, Mom and Dad standing by the chapel—me with a serious face swathed in a white headpiece, bandeau, and white veil, the rest of me covered in the long white habit and scapular, black leather belt, and the long rosary beads I'd dreamed about. After that, I did everything Sister Christine, the Novice Mistress, asked. I didn't like her. She was nothing like Sister Margaret Gerard, the Postulant Mistress, whose calm demeanor soothed our days. Instead, Sister Christine was mean.

Her voice bellowed across the meeting room. "Sisters, you are not worthy of the habit. You are a disgrace!"

She gave no reason for her tirade. She didn't need to. She was in charge and her word was final. I avoided her as best I could.

As novices, our choir stalls faced the new postulants. Ensconced in my novice outfit, I sat side by side with fourteen other novices who remained from the original twenty-eight from our band. As I chanted in Latin, I looked at the hymnal, then at the new postulants across from me. Our voices filled the chapel, rising into the vaulted ceiling, lifting in harmony:

Domine labia mea aperies et os meum adnuntiabit laudem tuam.

O Lord, open my lips and my mouth shall declare your praise.

I FELT AT peace as our voices floated above us in that space. After chanting, we meditated for a half hour before Mass. I still didn't know how to meditate—they never taught us how. So I prayed for several minutes, bowed my head, and asked God to make me a good Sister. The Sisters around me seemed to be experiencing a deep connection with God.

Or were they sleeping?

I had no idea that, after I entered the novitiate, I would lose touch with the Sisters I had admired. This included B.A.—Sister Beatrice Anthony, my sponsor—who wasn't allowed to write or visit me since she was a professed Sister. My world became very small. It would take years for me to reconnect with others and with myself.

When I entered the convent in 1967, I prayed like I had as a child—on my knees, head lowered. But now I was surrounded by Sisters instead of classmates in that voluminous chapel dedicated to Saint Agnes. We answered the priest who wore a golden chasuble (by then I knew the name of his priestly garment) that covered his white Dominican robe; I also knew the majority of the Latin prayers he called out, his back still turned to me, like the priests from my childhood.

God never spoke to me. Wasn't he supposed to if I was dedicating my life to him? I never asked my Sister friends if he spoke to them. Wasn't I in touch with my inner spirit in that time and sacred space?

My questions abounded. Questions like, *Who are you, God? Where are you? Are you in this community of Sisters who surround me? Are you really with me always?*

I carried these questions inside me, confiding with no one. This was personal. Something I needed to see through to the end. I believed God would reveal his plan to me. In time.

⟡

LIFE AS A novice surrounded me with mystery and ritual. Long rosary beads clicked when I walked, head lowered, hands folded, out of sight under the flowing scapular. I excelled in the art of pinning the veil atop a bandeau, the plastic piece that sat on my forehead and was attached to a tight, white cap that covered all my hair.

Still no television, radio, or newspapers. Spiritual books only. No hint of a war raging in Vietnam or peace protests, hippies sitting cross-legged on college campuses. No music from the Beatles, Simon and Garfunkel, or Sly and the Family Stone. Only Gregorian chant and Catholic hymns. Sister Grace with her red eyebrows disappeared to her next assignment while I rolled up my wide sleeves and tucked the scapular into my belt before I jockeyed a giant buffer over linoleum floors and ran the dishwasher in the steamy dish room.

Most of us continued to see our families once a month. As novices we only took poetry and theology classes rather than the full academic schedule we had taken as postulants. Perhaps they thought poetry and God would keep us holy. When we were told we could receive one Christmas gift from our family, I was excited. Even though I loved being Sister Kathleen Maura, who ignored her needs for a higher good, I also loved the idea of getting a gift. Parents were told they could deliver the gifts by Christmas Eve.

I sat on the edge of my bed as I read the list of approved gifts. It was short and tailored to spiritually serene novices and included sheets, towels, stationery, spiritual books. I had more than enough of those. Then an item toward the bottom caught my eye—a shawl. I had to think, what's a shawl? I'd never worn one. Then I remembered how professed Sisters clutched them like life jackets as they walked to the chapel in the frigid wind of Rockland County. I circled the word shawl, signed my name, and slipped the note under Sister Christine's door. I never thought, *Maura, you're nineteen years old. Ask for the newest Beatles album or* Teen *magazine.* No, a shawl would be perfect. When Sister Christine gave permission, I wrote my parents and asked for one.

It never dawned on me that asking in September for a shawl by Christmas was a huge request. How would they come up with one? How expensive would it be if they bought it? How much time would it take to knit one? I had no idea if Mom could knit. I knew Aunt Maggie did, but Mom? A part of me felt guilty even asking for a gift. The novitiate was training me well. "Empty yourself, commit yourself to God. Leave selfishness behind and you will be made whole." Was I being selfish by asking for it?

On Christmas Day we walked down to the chapel to chant, meditate, and attend high Mass, one that took longer than a regular Mass because of extra blessings and prayers. Darkness shrouded us as we walked. I pulled my black wool mantle tighter, wondering if a shawl would appear like my own Christmas miracle. The sun was up by the time we walked back to the motherhouse to serve breakfast to the professed Sisters. We had the day off from other chores, so I was free until we served another meal. I had no idea when I'd get my present.

Sister Christine, the Novice Mistress, was her usual self, staring daggers at me as I walked past her. *I don't know why she's so mad all the time*, I often thought. I closed the door to my room, sat on my bed, propped myself up against the pillow, and read about the life of another revered Dominican Sister, Saint Catherine of Siena. Everything was quiet, just the way I liked it.

Then the bell rang. I poked my head into the hall and saw Sister Christine clanging the hand bell up and down. This time of day was usually our quiet time, not a meeting time.

"Line up, Sisters. Line up in the hallway." I stood next to Kevin Francis, her forehead wrinkled in concern. I shrugged my shoulders. After Sister Christine counted us off, she led us down to the basement. Where were we going? There was nothing down here but the trunk room where Sister Christine threatened to send us if we talked after hours or malingered near professed Sisters. She knew how to scare us, slamming the keys to the trunk room on the desk, yelling, "Just take your trunk and go home."

I'd hold my breath, shake in my seat, and wait to hear my name. I thought I'd been good but with Sister Christine I never knew.

And now, where was she taking us? Halfway down the hall, past the trunk room, she pulled out keys and unlocked another door. When I stepped in, I was shocked. There in the corner was a Christmas tree trimmed in little white lights. And next to it Santa Claus stood, surrounded by gifts.

"Ho, ho, ho. Merry Christmas, Sisters. Come right over here. I have something for all of you."

With that, the deep-voiced Santa, who sounded a lot like Sister Marion, now a first-year professed Sister, waved us over. The helper Sisters who stood behind her smiled at us as we made our way toward the stacks of presents.

Santa sat down in a chair draped in a white sheet decorated

with Christmas garland and called us over one by one. When my turn came, I sat on Santa's knee like the other novices had done.

"Have you been good, Sister?"

"Very good, Santa."

"Well then, this must be for you." She handed me a box covered in wrapping paper. After the gifts were given out, we drank hot chocolate and ate cookies while Perry Como's "O Holy Night" and "Ave Maria" played on a boom box.

When I got back to my room, I opened my present. The shawl was gorgeous—delicate patterns in soft white wool with a Christmas card signed by my family. I pulled the shawl around me and read until it was time for dinner.

Two weeks later I got a letter from Dad. He was the main correspondent who kept me up on the family news. After he wished me Happy New Year, he wrote, "You might want to know the story of the shawl. Didn't Mom start knitting your shawl as soon as we received your letter. She had a few telephone consultations with Aunt Maggie, but she was sure she could get it done in time. From then on, I never saw her without her knitting bag. That shawl saw her through many a sleepless night until she dropped a cigarette and burned a hole in it. So off she was, knitting a new one, and, sure enough, didn't she finish that one at the start of December. It was then she thought, 'Let's give this shawl a quick rinse in cold water to soften it up.' And that's when a gremlin of some sort got to work because the shawl shriveled into an ugly mess.

"But you know your mother. She started on a new shawl, and this time nothing got in her way. Not sleep, not me, not those busy brothers of yours. Oh no. The shawl was done on Christmas Eve, just in time for me to deliver it. She would never tell you the story, but I thought I would." He signed it "Love, Dad" in his distinctive cursive swirl.

I was floored. The shawl I had wrapped around me wasn't just a gift. It was a miracle. And more than that, it was a symbol of Mom's unflinching stamina and love. A woman of few words, she showed her love for me in the soft wool wrapped around me.

⟡

WHEN I HAD free time, I walked to the cemetery behind the motherhouse. From the top of the hill, I could see beyond the novitiate, past the chapel and college, to the world that surrounded me. The elm trees rustled in the wind as I sat in solitude. No thinking. No words. A refuge from the constant demands of religious life. I wandered through the gravestones and wondered which row I'd be buried in when I died.

I brought my parents to the cemetery during one of their visits. "Dad and Mom," I said, pointing to the gravestones, "This is where I'll be buried when I die. You won't have to worry about taking care of that. Isn't that great?"

They shook their heads, more than likely aghast that their nineteen-year-old daughter reveled in the joy of owning her own gravesite.

⟡

AS A NOVICE, I was assigned to take care of the chapel. This was considered an honor, complete with ringing the chapel bell to gather the Sisters for prayers. Just before noon I went to the back of the vestibule, faced the locked door on the side wall, and selected a key from the key ring on my belt. I unlocked the door and stepped inside. My eyes traced the rope that hung from the bell high overhead in the steeple. I checked my watch. As the second hand swept past twelve, I took a breath, grabbed the rope in both hands, and pulled, bending my knees in a half genuflection.

Gong. In my head I repeated the opening lines of the Angelus, the prayer all of us said three times a day when I rang the bell. *The angel of the Lord declared unto Mary . . .*

Pause. Breathe. I pulled the rope again. Another gong. *And she conceived of the holy spirit . .*

I continued until I had rung the bell several more times and the Sisters had gathered in the chapel to pray. There was something magical about stepping into that enclosed space and pulling on the rope to honor Mary.

Working in the chapel also required me to prepare flowers for the altars.

"Every flower has a face." That's what Sister Christine said when she showed me how to arrange flowers for Mary's altar. After she showed me, she let me prepare flowers for Saint Joseph's altar which was across the aisle. He was Mary's husband, and his statue held a saw and a piece of wood because he was a carpenter.

"Every flower has a face. The important thing is to make sure you can see the face of each flower." Sister Christine pulled a stalk of red gladiola to the left, untangled a bunch of white carnations so they spread out in the vase. She turned to me and said, "Now, you do the next one."

My hands shook as I sorted through daisies with bright yellow petals. The purple iris smelled like grape soda and my tongue filled with saliva. I banished the thought, praying,

Forgive me, God. Help me to do the right thing. I gathered a few sprigs of fern, arranged them behind white calla lilies, paused, and moved a few steps away to make sure I could I see every flower.

I could feel Sister Christine's eyes burn through me, as if she knew I was lusting for grape soda. I wanted her to leave. When I turned to see if she was pleased, her cheeks were glowing in the spotlight that was shining on the altar. She had a Southern accent. I'd overheard Sister Albert Marie say Christine came from a posh school in Virginia. There was nothing posh here—just flowers and my shaky hands. Sister Christine nodded and left.

"Every flower has a face." Thanks to our head coverings and habits, only our faces and hands showed. Our faces were supposed to be lowered and, if we weren't working, our hands were to be folded in prayer, out of sight under the long white scapular that hung front to back. For those two years in the novitiate, I hid myself away and lowered my face so no one could see me.

As I write this is now, it seems that the real question is why did I enter the convent? Was it to follow the rules so well that I'd be chosen to arrange flowers in the chapel instead of clean toilets? Was it so I'd be rewarded for keeping silent and following the rules? I was nineteen years old, had never arranged flowers before, never gone on a date or kissed a boy.

Instead, I'd become Sister Kathleen Maura, putting my needs and wants aside to become a Sister who dedicated herself to God. It took a crisis about my father for me to raise my head, look Sister Christine in the eye, and find my voice.

◆

BY 1968, OF the twenty-eight who had entered the convent with me a year earlier, fourteen of us remained. Those who left had either been asked to leave or decided to leave. We never heard who had left for what reason. These Sisters simply disappeared and their rooms were cleaned out while we were off working or taking classes. Me? I kept out of trouble and avoided Sisters Albert Marie and Kevin Francis, who talked after lights-out or made jokes about Sister Christine. Sister Christine had a Jekyll and Hyde personality that ranged from a charming Southern belle façade, batting her eyelashes, to a screaming banshee who hurled an overladen key ring on the desk, shouting so loudly that the windowpanes rattled.

"None of you are worthy of the habit. None of you!"

Instead of sharing my worries about her erratic behavior, I spoke to no one. Talking with other Sisters would mean breaking the rule of keeping to oneself and praying all the time. I was determined to do what the Novice Mistress asked. I would be a good Sister. Little did I know that this would be the year I would help undermine Sister's Christine's reign of terror.

The two-year novitiate was a boot camp intended to form us into Sisters, to transform us from young girls into Dominican Sisters. It also sent home those deemed not ready to dedicate themselves to God. I wanted to stay. But even I reached a breaking point when Sister Christine went too far.

I didn't listen when Sister Albert Marie reported that she smelled cigarette smoke coming from Sister Christine's office. It couldn't be true. I put my head down and walked away.

But Albert Marie knew how to have fun and included me. Grand Silence, when no one was allowed to talk, started at night after lights-out. When we passed in the hall on the way to our rooms, Sister Albert Marie quietly said, "Tonight. Ice cream. Shower room. Midnight."

Ice cream? We're not supposed to . . . I paused. *Maura. Ice cream.* I couldn't resist. At midnight I tiptoed down the hall to the shower room with Sister Albert Marie and several others. We locked the doors, squeezed into two bathtubs, and huddled around tubs of ice cream, spoons raised. Albert Marie had "borrowed" the keys to the locked freezer and taken the ice cream. Eating that Neapolitan treat soothed any guilt I had about breaking the rules.

✧

THEN, SISTER CHRISTINE almost killed us.

A group of us joined her in the battered station wagon for a ride north. She got behind the wheel, sped out of the motherhouse, and screeched onto the Palisades Parkway, the road with steep drop-offs that curlicued along the edge of the Hudson River. She passed one car, then another, in a no passing zone. My stomach heaved as we tossed back and forth like cannonballs. Albert Marie turned to me, her face ashen. I squeezed her hand until we pulled into our destination. None of us knew what to do since Sister Christine ruled our lives. Somehow, we made it back to the motherhouse. None of us dared report her strange behavior, even though we knew something was very wrong with her. Novitiate forced us to obey her. We told no one what had happened.

A month later everything changed.

I was polishing silver spoons in the dishwasher room while waiting for Mom to call Sister Christine with news of

Dad's gallstone surgery. Each time I flipped a newly polished spoon into the soaking tub, I begged God to take care of him.

Then, Sister Christa Mary ran into the room, her cheeks flaming red. "Your mother called. Sister Christine yelled at her."

I dropped a spoon into the tub with a clink. "What do you mean? Why would Sister Christine yell at my mother?"

Christa Mary shook her head. "I don't know. She told your mother you were too busy to come to the phone."

She followed me as I yanked off the apron and walked as fast as I could down the hall to Sister Christine's office. She was at her desk as I surged through the door.

"Why did you yell at my mother?"

Her eyes widened, her lips narrowed into a frown. "Who told you?"

"It doesn't matter." I took a breath and spoke in a low growl. "How ... dare ... you. Don't you *ever* yell at my mother." Each word was a dart thrown dead center.

Her mouth fell open. "Why, Sister, you have left your family and ..."

"Sister Christine, you may have left your family, but I have not left mine. Get out of your office so I can call my mother back." I pointed to the door. "Now."

She stood up, straightened her scapular, and left. I picked up the phone and dialed the switchboard for an outside line. After a few rings, my mother answered. She started to cry as soon as she heard my voice.

"Maura, I'm so sorry I bothered you."

"Mom, I asked you to call. I'm sorry Sister Christine yelled at you. How's Dad?"

"I couldn't get any information from the hospital."

"Okay. I'll get down to see him and let you know what I find out." I'm not sure how I thought I'd do that since I was at the mercy of crazy Christine. I hung up and walked down to the main hall. Within minutes, the word had spread and the rest of the novices surrounded me. I broke down in tears as I told them what had happened.

A voice boomed from behind me. "What is the meaning of this? Sister Kathleen Maura, why are you crying?" I turned and faced the Mother General. Everyone scattered.

I told her everything. Her craggy face fell as she absorbed the news. She knew Dad, thanks to his volunteering. I reached out and took her hands in mine. "You must do something about Sister Christine. You must. There's something wrong with her. I need to see my father."

She looked at me, her eyes glistening with tears. "Go to your room and wait for me to arrange everything. Leave Sister Christine to me."

This was a turning point when I spoke my truth and overcame my fear of . . . what? Breaking rules? Ratting out the novice mistress who had serious issues? When Sister Christine yelled at my mother, I broke the veil of secrecy and intimidation that surrounded us and had frozen me into silence.

An hour later, Sister Albert Marie knocked on my door. "Sister Christine and I are going with you to see your father. Mother Evangelista signed out a car for us."

I was seething that Sister Christine had to come with us. But I had no choice if I wanted to see Dad. We walked to the switchboard to pick up the car keys. Before I turned on the ignition, I turned to Sister Christine. "I don't want to hear a word from you. When we get to the hospital, you will sit in the lobby and wait while we visit my father."

I drove down Route 9W along the Palisades Parkway over the Tappan Zee Bridge into the Bronx, praying the whole way. I remembered Dad driving the bus over this same bridge to show us the beauty of Christmas lights.

When we got to Bronx Lebanon Hospital, I parked, left Sister Christine in the lobby, and got on the elevator with Sister Albert Marie. A doctor with a nametag "Doctor Katter" got on with us. My mom had mentioned that was the name of Dad's doctor.

I turned to him. "Doctor, I'm Maura Doherty, Francis Doherty's daughter." He stared at me in my long white habit and veil and hesitated before he shook my hand. "Why don't we get off and talk for a minute?"

He and Albert Marie followed me off the elevator. "Doctor, how is my father?"

He looked at me.

"I need to know." My heart thudded as I asked the question a fellow novice had convinced me to ask. "How long does my father have to live?"

He let out a breath. "I just left him. He made me promise I would tell no one."

"Doctor," I said, holding up my scapular, "I don't get out much. You must tell me."

He fixed his eyes on mine, weighing his choices. In the next moment, he shattered my life. "Your father has colon cancer that has spread to his liver. How long does he have? Maybe six months, maybe a year."

I did everything not to scream, not to pound my fists on his chest. "Thank you, Doctor. I'll tell Dad I made you tell me." I took a breath and got back on the elevator. This was not the time to think or cry. When we got to Dad's room,

Albert Marie stayed by the door. Dad's bed was in the corner by the window. Outside, the Grand Concourse bustled with cars and buses and neighbors who lingered on park benches.

His eyes were closed.

"Dad? It's Maura."

He roused himself. "Maura, what are you doing here?"

"I just talked to the doctor."

He stared at me.

"I made him tell me."

My father looked at the ceiling and, after a minute, said, "Maura, I want to be like an ostrich and put my head in the sand."

I wanted to bury my head as well, pray his cancer away, and demand a miracle cure from Mary and her angels. Instead, I held his hand until it was time to leave.

✧

A FEW MONTHS after I saw Dad in the hospital, my brother Michael visited me at the motherhouse. It was the first time a family member had come on their own to see me. Michael was seventeen, two years younger than me. He'd taken the bus into the nearest town and walked a mile to the motherhouse. As we walked around the pond outside the novitiate, we chatted about how we were doing. We looked up as geese honked high overhead.

"It's beautiful here, Maura. I just wanted to get some time alone with you. It's weird when I come to see you with the family."

"I love that you came, Michael. Our family doesn't talk much, do they?"

A goose landed several feet away, followed by a few more. We paused and watched.

"No kidding," Michael said. The shoulder of his jean jacket had a peace symbol drawn in what looked like black marker pen. "Dad seems to be getting better. I'm glad."

I felt the ground shift under me. It dawned on me that he didn't know Dad was dying. I was the only one who did—aside from Dad. And he'd insisted that the doctor not tell the family. If I hadn't been so forceful, I wouldn't have known either.

I knew what I had to do. I looked at my brother. "Michael, Dad isn't going to get better. He has colon cancer that has spread to his liver. He may only have six or so months to live." I told him about my visit to the hospital and how I'd convinced the doctor to tell me the truth.

Michael's eyes flooded with tears. "It can't be true. It just can't be." He stared out at the pond as more geese joined the flock on the water. Ripples spread out until gentle waves touched the shoreline.

The enormity of what I had told him seemed to break something in him. He sagged against a nearby tree, his hand reaching out to grip the trunk as he stared at the pond. As if feeling his pain, the geese rose in a clatter of honks and thrashing wings and disappeared out of sight. If only our pain and the dreadful reality of Dad's illness would have been able to rise with them and find solace.

It didn't help that it was 1969. Many families of that era didn't learn the details of their loved ones' medical problems. Michael was the only sibling I told. And I didn't tell my mother. But by sharing the terrible truth with Michael, I'd found a way to break the silence of the secret Dad had bound me to.

For that, I am grateful.

AFTER I TOLD the Mother General about Sister Christine, she relieved Christine of her duties. Sister Margaret Gerard took charge of us again. Sister Christine was gone, as if we had imagined her. We never heard where she went, and I was glad she was out of our lives. I couldn't forget what she'd done to Mom and to all of us. Years later, when I walked through my own dark days, I remembered her and forgave her for how she had acted when she'd been stranded in a life that she hated.

But that was much later.

The rest of novice year was a blur of washing altars with bleach water, scrubbing toilets, and singing in the choir at funeral Masses for Sisters who died.

In Paradisum, deducant, te Angelei.
May the angels lead you to Paradise.

Dad underwent chemotherapy and looked decades older than his fifty-eight years when he came to visit me.

"I'm fine, Maura. Just tired."

However, there were no miracles, no heavenly intervention for him. He died six months later in the boys' bedroom with all the family around him. As my heart broke and his spirit left his body, the oak floors he had just installed glowed softly in the overhead light.

In Paradisum, deducant, te Angeli.

WHEN DAD GOT sick and Sister Christine yelled at my mother, I'd rebelled. I broke out of my "follow the rules at any cost" stance and pushed back. My inner spirit took charge when I asked for help from the Mother Superior. I took on Sister Christine and won. Even though I couldn't save my father, I spoke up and saved myself. My inner spirit, although bereft at his death, shone with clarity. God wanted me to be fully myself. Sister Kathleen Maura, on track to become a teaching Sister—a religious woman who tells the truth and fights for what is right. That was when I started to know what it meant to love God. First, I had to love myself and fight for those I loved.

✧

BEFORE DAD DIED, Mary Doreen and I were cleaning the novices' bathroom. As I scrubbed an immaculate toilet and Mary made half-hearted swipes at the sinks on the opposite wall, she called out, "Maura, I have an idea."

I flushed. "What, Mary?"

She always had ideas and questioned why we had to do things a certain way. "Why can't we get a subscription to the *New York Times*?" And, "Can't we listen to the news to find out what's going on with the Vietnam War?" When Richard Nixon was elected President, she was incensed. "He's a crook. He's a terrible person."

She was right about Nixon and a lot of other things.

But what I really wanted to say whenever she said that she had an idea was, "What now?"

"What did you say, Mary? I couldn't hear you over the toilet." I maneuvered the bucket and brush out of the stall.

She said, "I've been talking to the Sister in charge of

the college. We need a way to learn more than we're being taught here."

"She's a professed Sister, Mary. You shouldn't be talking to her."

There I was, the rule police telling her what she already knew, that professed Sisters were off-limits to us. I had no interest in changing colleges or improving my education. I just wanted to get my degree and start teaching.

"Maura, don't worry. She agreed that the college doesn't offer the upper-level courses we want. She told me we could transfer our credits to another college and still get our degree."

My heart thumped so loud I thought I'd have a stroke. My palms dripped with sweat, my head buzzed. "Mary, that's too much. I couldn't. You could. Not me."

A year later, after Mary and I finished our novice year, after my father got sick, after he died, after the world as I knew it came to an end, we did just that—transferred our credits to Fordham University (which was run by Jesuit priests) in the Bronx, where the two of us started life as "coed" Sisters in the undergraduate program.

Instead of closing the door to my room, hiding away from everyone and everything, Mary Doreen helped me open the door to the next chapter in my life as Sister Maura. Without her courage and tenacity, I might have stayed at the motherhouse, going to Saint Thomas Aquinas College and cleaning toilets.

✧

NOTHING WAS THE same after my father died. I was unmoored. The voice I had used to yell at Christine dried up as

I changed out of the long white habit into a knee-length one with a short veil. As I grieved the loss of my father, I took temporary vows of poverty, chastity, and obedience, promising to take permanent vows within seven years. I still wanted to be good, to do the right thing, but grief cut through me, slowed me down, haunted my dreams. More than ever, I needed the security of a solid community to support me.

Unfortunately, that didn't happen. In 1969, every community of Sisters was in an upheaval after Pope John XXIII and Vatican II urged religious women and men to move closer to the people they served. In fact, after Vatican II, *everything* Catholic changed. Vatican II, also called the Second Vatican Council, was a special meeting of Pope John XXIII and the Catholic bishops; it focused on re-evaluating the Church's mission. The Council lasted over three years. As a result of their work, altars were moved so priests faced the congregation; Latin prayers were replaced with English so we knew what we were saying. Religious women and men were urged to get closer to the people they served by changing not only where they lived, but also what they wore, and what they were called. They could now be called by their given name, not the name they took when they'd entered.

My community agreed. We were given the option to change from long habits into shorter ones with a modified veil that allowed some hair to show. At first, I resisted. How could they rob me of my dreams—the swish of the long white habit, the click of rosary beads, the name I had chosen to honor my mother? Instead of being called Sister Kathleen Maura, I could be called Sister Maura. Everything I had counted on was disappearing into the past.

I was crushed. How could this happen? I could have said

no. But the only Sisters who wanted to keep the longer habit were Sisters who refused to accept change. That wasn't me.

Was it?

I didn't want to be left behind so I did what my friends did; I changed into the short habit and veil, and renamed myself Sister Maura. The community moved away from a Mother General to a democratically elected president and community council. For many it was an exciting time. Not for me. Despite the outward changes, I felt lost. That year, hundreds of Sisters left the community including my sponsor, B.A., and Mary Doreen. The changes inspired by Vatican II led them to reconsider what they wanted to do with their lives. And they wanted out of the convent.

Night after night I lay in my bed crying for those who had left. Then, for myself.

What about me?
Who am I?
Do I still have a vocation?

six

EASTER

1970

AT AGE NINETEEN, I took temporary vows of poverty, chastity, and obedience. Vatican II had inspired our Sisters to change several key elements of religious life. Yes, I could invite my family to the ceremony where I'd "graduate" from the novitiate. Only now I would take what they called *temporary vows* or *promises*, not final vows. I would *promise* myself to God and to the community.

A promise? Wasn't that something I made to a friend?

Despite this, I couldn't wait to swear off money, sex, and making my own decisions—the opposite of what most women my age wanted. If I stayed vigilant, did the right thing, I'd be a college-educated Sister for the rest of my life. That was my goal. I had no idea what changes were coming my way.

I was assigned to work as a part-time "housemother" in Saint Agnes Home for Boys on the grounds of the motherhouse. The boys ranged in age five up to young adults, all from families in crisis who had been sent there from social service agencies in New York City. The orphanage was in a sprawling set of buildings that included an ancient five-story building with turrets plucked out of a gothic novel. The boys were separated by age into groups housed in dormitories with beds lined up along the wall. Since our community was a teaching order, the Sisters provided schooling up to the eighth grade, then transferred the boys to local high schools. My job included helping with after-school programs.

I didn't think about what living in a large orphanage in suburban Rockland County was like for these city kids. But there they were and so was I. I knew little about the boys assigned to me. But, thanks to having four brothers, I knew enough about boys to get by. They were pretty well-behaved but called out when they weren't happy.

"Cheap man, welfare," was their rallying cry if they thought they'd been mistreated.

One boy yelled, "Eduardo got more dessert than me."

The rest of the group would call out, "Cheap man, welfare."

Another shouted, "Ernie used up all the hot water."

"Cheap man, welfare," was the response.

I talked to each of them as they rotated between classes and group assignments. They tolerated me as just another Sister who'd cycle in and out of their lives, even if I was fairly good at running bases and catching flyballs.

One boy, Kevin, an eleven-year-old, rarely complained and kept to himself. But he catapulted off home plate after hitting one home run after another—as if speed would make up for living in a group home far from the city.

I didn't question where "home" was for me. It was back at 1210 Olmstead Avenue in the Bronx, a stone's throw from the noisy Cross Bronx Expressway. The motherhouse was a temporary place to learn more about being a Sister and prepare me to become a teacher. When I signed out a car so I could have Easter dinner with my family in the Bronx, I was going home. It would be the first Easter without Dad.

Kevin was the only boy in my group who had nowhere to go. The other boys had friends or relatives taking them out for the day. I was conflicted. The Sisters would take care of him, but I didn't want to leave him behind. I screwed up my courage and asked the Sister in charge if I could take Kevin with me. After she agreed, I called my mother, who also said, "Yes."

"Kevin, I'm going to Easter dinner with my family in the Bronx. Would you like to come with me? The food should be pretty good."

He paused, then nodded.

That's how Kevin and I found ourselves driving down the Sprain Brook Parkway to the Bronx. The car was like the one I had driven Mother Kevin in when I'd been a postulant—a four-door luxury sedan with plush leather seats. This time I knew where I was going. While I thought about my father and how it would be without him, Kevin stared toward the apple and cherry blossoms in full bloom on the side of the road.

It wasn't until I rang the bell and saw my mother's face that I remembered something. Kevin was Black. My family was White. My mother stared at him. I realized that, until that point, no person of color had entered our home. It had never dawned on me since my life now included so many people from different backgrounds. I stood up straighter and trusted she'd treat him well. She led us inside and introduced him to my siblings. Kevin watched as we added extra leaves to the table in the TV room and laid out the Irish linen tablecloth, Franciscan Rose China, and sterling silver. My brother

John entertained him with card tricks as we put out the food. Despite the expanded table, we sat elbow to elbow in that small room. Three brothers and Kevin sat across from me at the table: one Black face amidst a sea of White ones. As we said grace, I blinked back tears when I noticed that my oldest brother, Francis, was sitting in Dad's chair at the head of the table. The roast lamb, twice-baked potatoes, and green beans were delicious, but I had a hard time enjoying the meal. Dad was missing. Forks and knives scraped on plates as my brothers chatted with Kevin.

Michael asked, "What do you do for fun, Kevin?"

After Kevin took a sip of milk, he said, "We play baseball and sometimes we sing."

"Do you have any favorite songs?"

Kevin shook his head.

Mom asked if he wanted seconds. "No, thank you. I'm pretty full."

As I helped clear the table, I glanced out the window. It was snowing. A blizzard. By the time we finished dessert, the snow was several inches deep and still coming down. Kevin and I weren't going anywhere that night. I called the motherhouse to let them know we'd stay here overnight. Mom led us into the front room where she had Easter baskets for everyone, including Kevin.

"For me?" he asked as his eyes grew wide.

"Yes, for you, Kevin."

I don't think he'd ever seen so much chocolate.

He sat in the boys' bedroom reading a book while we finished putting away leftovers. As I opened the refrigerator, I heard his sweet voice singing Michael Jackson's "I'll be There." He sat alone in that room singing what might have been his favorite song in soft tones that matched the quiet snowfall that surrounded us. He had found a moment of peace amidst that unfamiliar household.

Mom lent him a pair of pajamas and asked if he'd like to take a bath.

"A bath? Sure."

"I'll get it ready for you. "

An hour later Mom's whispered to me, "Is he okay in there?" pointing to the bathroom door just a few feet away.

"He's fine, Mom."

"He's awfully quiet, Maura."

"Okay, I'll check on him."

I knocked lightly. "Kevin, how are you doing?"

"Okay."

"Take your time."

He emerged a short time later, his face shining. He announced he was ready for bed.

Mom fixed us breakfast the next morning—scrambled eggs, sausage, and toast along with her special jam tarts. Kevin thanked her, said goodbye to everyone, and seemed relaxed as we started the drive back. The roads had been plowed and sanded and the newly blossomed trees were covered in snow.

About halfway there, I asked, "Kevin, how was the visit with my family?"

"Okay."

I wondered if he'd tell the other boys about his adventure. After a minute he let out a long sigh and turned to me.

"Sister, that's the first bath I ever had."

I thought about the communal showers in the dorms, how dozens of boys shared them. "Is that so, Kevin? How was it?"

He sat back, stretched out his legs, and smiled. "Real good."

That lifted my spirits. Dad would have loved Kevin and would have wanted him to eat at our table. Even if Dad wasn't there in person, I wondered if he might have sent the snow so we'd spend the night and Kevin could have his first bath. Perhaps Kevin had found a temporary refuge in my home, a place where we shared a meal, chocolate, and a chance for him to take a long, hot bath surrounded by the beauty of snow.

At that time, I was happy with my life as Sister Maura. Years later, though, I was the one who needed refuge from my life as a Sister. Friends helped me with a place to stay and, later, with my transition to a new city where I could leave the trappings of religious life behind. I hope Kevin had friends who helped him along the way as well.

seven

TEACHING

WHEN I TOOK a vow of obedience, it seemed straightforward. I would be obedient if I did everything my superiors asked. But reality set in when I was assigned to my first mission, the name for where we were sent to work after the motherhouse. Even with forward-thinking leadership, they sent me to teach third grade at an elementary school in the Bronx. Third grade? I knew nothing about young children. I was twenty years old, fresh out of the novitiate, working on a degree in biology. I'd asked to teach high school science. I assumed I would know how to teach that since I knew the coursework. They responded by charging me with teaching eight-year-olds. A pit burned in my stomach. How could they do this to me? My vow of obedience meant I had no option. I had to swallow my fear, forge ahead, and do what my superiors ordered.

A few weeks before school started, I put on my shortened habit and veil, packed my bag, got a ride, and rang the bell at Saint Brendan's convent. The neighborhood around Saint Brendan's school, north of the Bronx Zoo and Fordham University, included red brick apartment buildings and narrow duplexes. The church, built in 1960, sat next to the school. Its front façade was a majestic sweep of creamy brick shaped into the prow of a ship in honor of Saint Brendan, whom many believe sailed from Ireland to North America long before anyone else. The convent was next to the church, and it was where I went first.

A Sister wearing a long habit opened the door.

"Yes?"

"I'm Sister Maura. I'll be teaching third grade."

"You're expected. Come this way." She guided me along a long corridor that had many closed doors; halfway down, she stopped. "This is your room." I felt my heart sink as she nodded and left me there, her footsteps barely making a sound as she disappeared down the hall.

My room was like the one in the novitiate—a twin bed, sink, desk, and chair, and a crucifix on the wall. After taking a few minutes to unpack, I returned to the hall and wandered a little, finding the living room, kitchen, and dining room. Then I walked into the school, found the third-grade classroom with my name on the door, and started to decorate bulletin boards. I guessed that eight-year-olds liked color so I chose the brightest poster boards I could find in the supply closet and decorated them with titles like "Math," "Spelling," "Penmanship." Next, I took the textbook and returned to my room to prepare. *I can do this*. I had no idea how to handle such young students, let alone how to teach them anything.

Over the next few days, I met the other Sisters as we gathered for meals. Conversation was minimal, and most of us returned to our rooms each evening to prepare classes. I was too insecure to talk with these women who had decades of teaching experience.

I studied the third-grade textbook like it was the Bible, preparing lesson after lesson. On the first day, teachers and students gathered in the schoolyard. I held up a sign for the third-grade, and a cascade of students—fifty of them—lined up behind me. I led them into the classroom where I placed them in rows in alphabetical order. I acted like I knew what I was doing despite my hammering heart and sweaty palms. The students were well-behaved and did everything that I asked.

A PHOTO FROM that time shows several students sitting at their desks bent over workbooks, pencils in hand. One girl is looking at the camera, her long brown hair tied in a red ribbon. Did she know my secret, that I didn't know how to teach?

My classroom was across the hall from the first grade taught by Sister Stephen Gerard. I could tell from sounds that echoed from that room that she loved her students. I didn't love mine. They terrified me. They looked at me and waited to be told what to do. Every day, I got to school early, laid down yellow number two pencils and a ruler, and opened the textbook. Beyond that, I followed the bare-bones lesson I'd sketched out the night before. I'd never taken a teacher education class. In 1970, Sisters who'd been hired by Catholic schools weren't required to be certified as teachers. But because they were Sisters, anything they said or did was all right in the Church's eyes.

I don't remember how things came to a head. Maybe it was after another Sister said that third grade was crucial for teaching students how to write in cursive. How was I supposed to do that? All I had to go on was one textbook and vague memories of my own time in third grade. Partway through the school year, I walked into Sister Stephen Gerard's classroom and said, "I need help."

She looked at me from behind thick, black-framed glasses and asked, "What do you need help with?"

"Everything." I burst into tears. To this day I wonder if it was desperation or fear of failure that drove me to her. Maybe both.

She stood up. "Why don't you show me what subject you're working on?" She followed me to my classroom where I choked back tears and opened the book to the current lesson.

"What does the teacher's manual say about this chapter?" Her voice was gentle.

"Teacher's manual?" I had no clue what that was.

"Oh," she said. She walked over to the bookshelf and picked out a thicker version of the book on the desk.

"Here," she said, placing it next to the open one. "This tells you how to plan your lesson." She ran her finger along red highlights down the side of the page.

I stared at it. "I didn't know." My voice trailed off as tears rolled down my cheeks.

She patted my hand. "It's all right. I'll help you."

I met with her several days a week to prepare lessons and review homework. She was a patient mentor, and our one-on-one sessions went smoothly. Inside I was seething and humiliated. Every day after that, I stood in front of those students as Sister Maura, more prepared than I'd been before, but painfully aware of how stupid I felt. I made it through the year, always sealing myself in my room after school to hide my frustration.

On the last day of school, I waved goodbye to students and their parents, who still believed that Sisters were always right. I knew better. My hand shook as I stashed their gifts in a brown paper bag and placed it in a closet. My face flushed with rage. How dare they assign me to a job I wasn't qualified for? I thought of the students' trusting faces as I'd led them through their lessons. Never again would I allow myself to be put in that position. I had to do the right thing for myself first. I would not allow my vow of obedience be blind obedience to an antiquated rule. I cared for myself and my students too much to let that happen again.

But what changes could I make to make this reality? I looked down at the shortened habit I wore as an outward sign of my vows. *That's it*, I thought. I could change what I wore to symbolize my commitment to honor my new resolve.

After Vatican II we had the option to wear regular clothes instead of the habit. Many of my Sister friends had changed into lay clothes—a black skirt and a white blouse. But I had not yet done that. That day, however, I went back to my room in the convent, hung up my habits and veils, put on my new clothes, and slammed the closet door.

And I promised myself that if the community assigned me to teach elementary school again, I would say no.

That didn't happen. That summer I was told to report to Aquinas High School to teach biology. Finally, a subject I knew. But the next challenge was deciding where to live. We now had the option of choosing where we wanted to live—whether it be in a traditional convent, an apartment, or other living arrangement.

What was I going to do?

eight

ALPHA HOUSE

WHEN I ENTERED the order in 1967, there was one option of where to live after the novitiate—in a convent like Saint Brendan's. In post-Vatican II, however, our community supported us if we chose more creative living arrangements. Mary Doreen introduced me to two Sisters who were starting Alpha House, a halfway house for women from prison in a large three bedroom, two bath apartment in the West Bronx. It sounded like a good idea. Why not live with two other Sisters who were helping other women? When I visited the Sisters, any doubts I had dissolved. They were down-to-earth, rooted in religious life, and eager to start this new program. I was ready.

"Alpha" was the perfect way to describe a new beginning not only for the residents, but also for me. I packed my suitcase, the same one I'd carried when I entered the order. Now, however, I carried it to the west side of the Bronx, away from Saint Brendan's and my struggles with third grade.

Alpha House could house up to three residents in addition to three Sisters. The two who started it—Sisters Ann and

Anne Marie—had been in the convent for several years. I was still new, unsure of what religious life meant. How was it that I trusted them even after finding out that I'd share a bedroom with one of the residents? My stomach was in knots when I met my roommate, Joyce. She had lustrous long, black hair, and a voice inflected with the lilt of Trinidad. The peace that emanated from her calmed me. Maybe it would be okay that we shared a bedroom. Another resident, Peggy, had a single room down the hall. After a few days Joyce and I settled into a pattern of waking up in time to share breakfast with the two other Sisters before Joyce took the train downtown to an office job. The roiling in my stomach settled as I rode the #36 crosstown bus to teach at the high school.

One weekend when the others were out, Joyce said, "Sister, I will show you how to make coconut bread." She reached for bowls, gathered ingredients, then pulled a hairy brown globe from a grocery bag. This was something I'd never seen before. "First, the coconut." She put it on the counter and cracked it open with a hammer. She showed me how to grate each piece to get out the most meat. When she and I both cut our fingers on the sharp edges of the grater, she said, "That is our love going into the bread. My mother told me the red blood is the love we share with those who eat our bread. Now," she said, "both of us will share our love with the others."

I thought about how little I'd learned from Mom and her flawless apple pies and jam tarts, and how I wished I'd learned more. I continued grating the coconut and adding a bit more love into the bowl, red subsumed into the white, disappearing when we folded it into the batter. Love and story. That is what I learned from Joyce.

My failure as a third-grade teacher faded in that cozy

kitchen with the mouthwatering aroma of fresh coconut bread. All of it was in stark contrast to the year I'd lived at Saint Brendan's, where solemn Sisters lived and prayed together and returned to their rooms to get ready for another day of teaching. They repeated the cycle day after day. Convent life in the motherhouse and Saint Brendan's had worked for them. But not for me.

Sisters Ann and Anne Marie were easy to live with. Their goal was to give women who'd just been released from prison a safe place to live while they got their feet on the ground, found work, and re-entered society. Both of the Sisters taught science at Cathedral High School in Manhattan. Our residents would be home during the day until they found jobs and moved to a place of their own. Until then, we lived together as a quasi-family, sharing stories about our day, and supporting each other as best we could.

For one of our residents, Peggy, this wasn't easy. All she wanted once she got out of jail was to skip Alpha House and return to her friends. I can see how living with three Catholic Sisters and former convicts might have felt like a hardship. She was young, all of twenty, with bleached blonde hair with an insistent swath of brown roots that crept out of her scalp. She stayed in her room most of the time and, after persistent coaxing, helped with meals. I have a vague memory that she'd been arrested for forging checks. Whatever it had been, it was enough to get her arrested and released into our care. She could stay as long as she played by the house rules. But it turned out that wasn't for her.

In order for us to protect the privacy of our residents, none of them were allowed visitors from friends or family unless the Sisters agreed. This worked well for everyone—except

Peggy. One day when I arrived home, I heard voices coming from her bedroom. I knew that everyone was out, so I knocked on her door and asked, "Peggy, do you have company?"

No answer.

"Peggy?"

I heard muffled voices.

"Please open your door, Peggy."

She came out with a young man called Tony. Tall, with slicked back hair, shiny leather jacket, and skintight jeans,

"Sister Maura, my friend came to visit."

"Peggy, you know the rules. No visitors. Tony, you'll have to leave."

His mouth pulled into a slit.

Peggy looked at him, said, "Sorry," and went back into her room as I led him away.

Partway down the hall, his muscled build towered over me when he wheeled around and snarled, "This isn't right. Peggy's my friend."

Chills ran down my arms. I was on my own. If he attacked me, I was in trouble. "House rules, Tony. No visitors." Could he feel my heart pounding? Did he see my hands shaking as I kept walking? I needed to get him out of the apartment.

Before we got to the door, he swung around again, that time with a knife in his hand, pointed at me. "No. I'm not going."

I'd never experienced an adrenaline rush before. I knew from biology it triggered a fight-or-flight instinct. I didn't flee. Instead, I reached up, grabbed both of his hands, slammed him against the wall, twisted the knife away, unlocked the door, threw him into the vestibule, and locked the door behind him. Like a scene from the movie "Sister Act." Adrenaline had given all five-foot-five inches of me the strength to grab the knife and boost him out the door. I had never worked out and had little strength in my arms. And though he rammed himself against the door several times, the door held. When he left, I ran back inside, grabbed the phone, dialed 9-1-1, and waited for the police. That's when I noticed blood running down my hand—the hand that had grabbed the knife. My daredevil act had sliced open the fleshy part at the base of my thumb. I grabbed a towel, put pressure on it, and sat down at the kitchen table where every part of me shook.

Peggy cracked open her door. "Sister Maura, are you okay?"

"Stay in your room, Peggy. Don't even think about coming out."

The police arrived within minutes and were shocked to learn that we were running a halfway house on their beat.

Officer O'Connor, stared at me. "What you did was very dangerous, Sister." His voice shook, like he couldn't believe what had happened. "How long have you lived here? We should have known so we could watch out for you."

"We've been here about a year. We wanted to keep a low profile to protect the privacy of our residents."

I sat down again, still shaky from what had happened. The police then checked the windows to make sure they were secure, questioned Peggy, and were taking my statement as the other Sisters arrived home. After I told them what happened, the officers gave us their contact information in case we needed help in the future.

Tony never showed his face again.

His knife had "007" etched on its wooden handle. I later learned that this switchblade was popular in crime-ridden

New York in the 1970s and was called a "flick knife." The five-inch, extra-sharp blade opened with the flick of the wrist. No wonder I never saw it coming. All Tony had to do was pull it out of his pocket to expose the blade. I was lucky. Accounts of 007 knife attacks are filled with victims who sustained horrific injuries that required hundreds of stitches. Many of them did not survive.

Years later, after I left the convent, and after my time in Alpha House, I remembered how, at first, I'd resisted change and followed the rules. Then how I began to see how others were changing. I wanted to be like them. Friends like Sisters Ann and Anne Marie showed me how to help others in a close, intimate setting. Thanks to them and other friends, I learned that resistance to change didn't work. Change would happen anyway. Change came despite my not wanting it. If I hadn't changed, I might have missed out on some amazing adventures. Thanks to my Sister friends, life opened for me in ways I'd never imagined.

The day of the incident with Tony wasn't the last time we saw Officer O'Connor. Late one night he called to ask us to help a woman who needed protection from her abusive husband. "She's scared. But no place will take her until morning. Is there any chance she can stay with you until I get her to the shelter?"

We said yes. That night she slept on our couch and shared breakfast with us before Officer O'Connor drove her to the shelter. Thanks to Tony, we were able to help another woman in need.

✧

SOON AFTER PEGGY moved out, Norma moved in. She was referred to us from the psychiatric wing of a prison in Queens. I was a full-time student at Fordham. If I hadn't been studying in that kitchen at Alpha House, memorizing Latin nomenclature, genus, and species, and creating mnemonics to memorize thousands of muscles and classes of bacteria, I'd never have gotten to hear Norma's story.

Norma was quiet. Much of the time she stayed in the room with the door closed. Since I had little space to spread out my books except on my bed or at the kitchen table, I studied in the kitchen where Norma crafted her magic.

My classes at Fordham were in the morning, so most afternoons found me at the kitchen table. Sunlight spilled through the window as I poured over the textbook *Chordate Morphogenesis*, my notebook filled with notes about synapomorphies and notochords.

When Norma came in to start dinner, we nodded to each other, and continued our work. She put on a red flowered apron that emphasized her large frame, then reached for mixing bowls, flour, salt, butter, and eggs. She lined up the ingredients and turned to me, her eyes magnified through thick glasses. "Sister Maura, maybe today you want ravioli, not the spaghetti? Ravioli with spinach, some with meat, some the cheese?" Her Italian accent reminded me of my Italian neighbors from Olmstead Avenue.

"Norma, make whatever you want. I love your cooking." I thought about the ravioli Mom served back home, Chef Boyardee with Ragu sauce. I knew that Norma's would be better than that.

She turned her back to me, went to the counter, reached for the flour, then faced me again. "I think, today, all kind of ravioli."

Over the next few hours, as I perused microbiological drawings of cocci and spirochetes, Norma sifted and mixed, kneaded, rolled, and cut out pasta dough in rectangles that were big enough but not too big. As she simmered garlic and onions, my stomach growled with anticipation. She added spinach until the mixture looked just right. Shredded beef piled up on the cutting board, more onions and garlic went into the skillet along with oregano and thyme, then the meat. At this point all I could do was stare and salivate. She moved as if she was conducting a symphony. The aromas made the sketches of microorganisms seem to lift off the page, entranced by the feast to come.

My admiration for her grew in that kitchen as she stuffed the ravioli and creased the edges with a fork. Later, she toiled over boiling pots of water as her pasta creations bounced up and down until she fished them out and laid them in a bowl. Bringing it all together was blood red sauce, a symbol of the alchemy that gave the meal life, sometime ravioli, other times, spaghetti Bolognese, veal parmesan, or baked ziti.

All because of Norma.

As she prepared each meal, I found my way to her, luxuriating in her presence as a way to counteract the lifeless studies in front of me. Her artistry softened the edges of my life as a student and opened me to the joy of watching her come to life in the kitchen.

As time went on, she shared bits and pieces of her story, like a progressive dinner served over weeks and months.

"Bobby, my son. Such a good boy," she said one afternoon while she stuffed shells, tears coursing down her cheeks. Then she transferred the pasta to the baking pan as she waited for the oven to heat. When she was finished, she sat and sipped a glass of water. She offered no further details about her son; the mere mention had been enough for now.

Days later, as she pounded chicken cutlets to tender filets, she turned to me, her apron spotted with butter and flour. "Bobby was so good. Until he met those boys. Bad boys." She walked toward me, gripped the edge of the table, and leaned over, as if the burden of her story was weighing her down. "He stole from me. Stopped going to school. Stayed out all night. Came home drunk. High. Yelling things no mother should hear." She lifted her head and looked right at me. "Why, Sister Maura? Why did he do these things?" Then, she returned to the cutting board to pound more chicken, raised the mallet, then smashed it down as if it was responsible for what had happened.

Weeks later, scalloped potatoes lay under cream and cheese, when Norma suddenly said, "My Bobby stole the rent money. *Our* rent money." A flood of tears washed down her face. "Why, Sister Maura? How could this happen?" She took a breath, turned, opened the oven door, and slid the tray inside, the heat coursing into the kitchen, as if she herself was on fire. Both of her hands began to close the oven, the bulk of her facing away from me as she raised the door inch by inch, as if shutting away the parts of the story she had not yet shared. Then the door shut with a click, and she left the kitchen.

I didn't know what to say. I had no answers. I could answer all the questions in my textbooks, but I had no answer for her.

All I could do was listen.

Over the next month, as I reached the end of the semester, Norma and I peeled carrots, their brilliant orange pulsating in olive oil. "My Bobby broke my heart," she blurted out one night. "The priest, he tell me, 'Pray, Mrs. Morigi.' I say, 'I pray all the time, Father.' He say, 'Pray harder, Mrs. Morigi.'"

We cut tender eggplant and rolled each slice in egg and breadcrumbs before she put them into the oven. Love mixed into each dish, baked into each meal as if it could relieve her pain.

"One night Bobby yelled so loud, it hurt my ears. Then, nothing. I remember nothing after that. It was like the switch in my brain turned off, Sister Maura." She stared at me, one hand clenching the back of the chair until her knuckles turned white. Her eyes were vacant, as if she'd been transported back to an apartment in Queens where she'd faced her son. Then she shuddered, the chair shaking as she grasped it. "They tell me I killed him, my Bobby. That I stabbed him and jumped out the window to kill myself." She shoved the chair away from her like it was to blame. Then, her eyes found mine. "Only, he is dead, and I am not." She held out her right arm, angry red scars running the length of it, as she stared at an imprint of pins and plates that pieced her arm together.

"I pray to God for forgiveness." She looked at me, her eyes blurred behind her glasses as she took a seat across from me. "I remember nothing from that night. But I know one thing—my Bobby will never forgive me." With that, she reached into her apron pocket and pulled out rosary beads, slipping them through her fingers, her lips moving in silent prayer.

I prayed with her at that table, the Hail Marys and Our Fathers asking angels to surround her with love, with forgiveness, with peace.

We grew closer that year, bonded by hours in that kitchen,

much of it in silence as she laid out pasta in orderly rows, as if that would heal her trauma, soothe her broken heart.

One afternoon she rolled pot roast in a bed of herbs then slid it into the pan. "I don't remember what happened that night, Sister Maura. I know Bobby is dead. But I don't know what happened. The doctor says sometimes when things get bad, the brain, it shuts down." She dusted off her hands, placed the meat in a baking dish, added some stock, and put it in the oven. Heat and the aroma of beef and spices filled the kitchen as we waited for it to cook.

YEARS LATER, A friend of mine told me how one Sunday morning, she'd woken up at her kitchen table, the newspaper open in front of her, a fresh croissant on a plate, and coffee cooling in her cup. Her bed was made, two throw pillows angled just the way she liked them. But she had no memory of getting out of bed or driving to the bakery several blocks away. She checked the car for damage. There was none. All she remembered was going to bed the night before, exhausted from months of traveling across the globe for work. She took a week off, and saw her doctor.

"This happens sometimes," he said. "We lose our memory when stress takes over and pushes everything aside. Do what you can to reduce your stress and your mind will recover."

She resigned from her job and left it all behind. Now she works at a low-stress job and paints canvases filled with vibrant reds and yellows, blues, and greens. To this day she has no recollection of what had happened during those lost hours. Thankfully, it never happened to her again.

ALTHOUGH I NEVER experienced stress-induced memory loss like Norma and my friend, within a few years I suffered my own stress-related health problems. It wasn't until years later that I realized how pushing myself to the limit could have a serious impact on my health.

At the time, I had no idea how precious those hours with Norma were. How my heart opened to compassion and forgiveness as my thumb and index finger caressed the beads, counting off another decade of the rosary. The Sorrowful, Glorious, and Joyful mysteries wrapping Norma and me and our fellow residents in a sonata of prayer. But as I prayed, the very foundation of our religious life was crumbling. Hundreds of Sisters were choosing to leave the convent after Vatican II asked them to rededicate themselves to the poor and suffering.

✧

THEN, I FOUND a job for Norma. Alpha House required residents to work. We helped as best we could, matching them with employment counselors and job opportunities. Norma's skills were in the kitchen. She was still recovering from the trauma she had suffered. Where might she find a good place to work?

One Sunday I sat next to my mother in church in my home parish. Mom's head was bent in prayer, rosary beads running through her fingers as we waited for Mass. This was the church where I had been baptized, received Holy Communion, gone to school taught by the same community of Sisters I joined years later. I opened the church bulletin and spotted a posting for a job as the rectory cook and housekeeper.

Norma, I thought. Then, *No, the priests can't have her. I need her.* She was my lifeline. Her smile lit up the room when I returned from school. She celebrated me with special desserts each time I finished final exams. I didn't want her to cook for scrawny Father Dee, whose voice squeaked like a mouse when he preached from the pulpit, or for Father Colby, whose sweat soaked through his robes as he greeted parishioners. But as Mom tucked the rosaries into her purse, I knew what I had to do. I had to tell Norma about the job.

After I got back to Alpha House and the other Sisters agreed that it was a good idea, I handed Norma the paper. She read it, lowered it to her side, and said, "No."

"No?" I asked.

"No. I am not good enough to cook for priests."

I took a breath. "Norma, they would be lucky to have you. Why don't you think about it?"

The next day she called them and when she returned from the interview, she beamed. "Those priests, they have such a nice stove. But I will need my own apartment."

And so, my friend Norma, who made cooking an art form, whose story filled the kitchen with sorrow and remorse and love, moved to an apartment just two blocks from my family home in the Bronx.

She and I had spoken about so many things—how the weather had turned cold; how the buds were blooming on the camellia bush outside the front door; how our fellow resident, Joyce, made the best coconut bread. We shared many hours of silence as she worked her magic in the kitchen. When she moved out, I lost something beyond words. The pain inside me cut through my gratitude that she was moving on in her life. But nothing felt the same.

Every week we got a phone call from her, telling us how she was and how she liked having more people to cook for, but she always insisted she missed us very much.

ONE SUNDAY AFTER Mass as Mom and I left the parish church, I spotted Norma walking toward us. She and I hugged before I turned to Mom.

"Mom, this is my friend, Norma. Norma, this is my mother, Kathleen Doherty."

Norma beamed and reached out to shake my mother's hand. "Mrs. Doherty, I'm so glad to meet you. Your daughter is such a good person. She helped me so much." Her face beamed with delight.

We said goodbye and Mom and I walked home, Mom asked me, "How do you know her?"

Without thinking I said, "I met her at Alpha House."

Weeks later, on one of my visits, my mother was washing dishes when she turned around and said, "Maura, that woman said to say hello."

"What woman, Mom?" It took me a few minutes to realize whom she meant. "Do you mean Norma? The woman who works in the rectory?"

"Oh, Maura. Really." She shook her head and turned back to washing dishes.

"Mom, Norma is my friend. I would appreciate it if you would at least say her name."

The running water muffled the "Humph" from Mom as she rinsed the last dish, put it in the rack, and left the kitchen.

Did Mom refuse to say Norma's name after she'd learned her connection with Alpha House, a home for women from prison? Was Mom angry that I'd brought Norma into her church and neighborhood? Was she afraid of Norma? I didn't know. No matter what Norma's past was, she deserved respect.

I followed Mom into the TV room. "Mom, can we talk?"

She sat down in her armchair and turned on the television. "Enough, Maura." She turned up the volume. Over the blaring commercial I heard her say, "I'll never understand you."

Fear can do that—shut us down when we feel scared. When I feared the barrage of changes that swept through the convent, I shut down. I had assumed habits, veils, religious names, our very way of life, would always be there, would keep me safe. I would be Sister Kathleen Maura clad in the traditional habit with long rosary beads. I would be happy. When I'd realized that all my Sister friends, women I admired, were making radical changes in how they dressed, where they lived, and the very names they went by, I hadn't wanted to be left behind. I was not a trailblazer. I was a follower. Maybe Mom needed peers who would listen to her feelings about Norma. Maybe if her friends offered her another approach, Mom could begin to accept Norma's presence in the neighborhood. And maybe even accept my friendship with her.

The next time I was in the neighborhood, I pressed the bell to the rectory and Norma answered the door. "Oh, Sister Maura, come in, come in." She put her finger to her lips, took my hand, led me down the hall, and pointed to a chair at the kitchen table.

"How is everything, Norma?" I inhaled the tantalizing aroma of tomato sauce.

She grabbed my hands. "Sister, I am so happy you come to visit. How are the other Sisters?" She looked over her shoulder and lowered her voice. "The priests, they're not fun like you Sisters, but they okay. There's one who can't eat so much because of his sugar—no pasta for him," she whispered. "And the other one, tch, tch," she wrinkled her nose. "Oh, that one, he not so easy. But what you gonna do?" With that she laughed.

We talked some more before I left. The squeak of her crepe soles was muffled by the thick red carpet as we made our way down the hall to the front door. We kept in touch for years.

I thought I was helping Norma find a better life. As Sister Maura, I was compassionate and forgave her for what she'd done. Years later I realized *she* had taught me about compassion. I had compassion for her as she grieved her part in killing her son. Then, when I faced my own dark days, I remembered Norma and had compassion for myself.

nine

AQUINAS HIGH SCHOOL

IN 1967, THERE were over 900 of us in the community before the freedom offered by Vatican II decimated our ranks. Five years after I entered the convent, I swallowed my heartbreak as Alpha House closed and the two Sisters who had started it left the convent along with hundreds of other Sisters. At the time I had no idea the toll that these departures had on me. My heart was hurting, and I was losing confidence in religious life. I'd become a Sister to help others in community with other Sisters. That dream was disintegrating as, one after another, my lifelines and Sister friends disappeared.

After Alpha House closed, I moved into the convent at Aquinas High School with ten other Sisters. Might this become my new home, my new community? We were together in this. The knot in my throat eased as we sat in silent meditation in the chapel and I prayed to adapt to this traditional convent.

God was the focus, but God as in the universal, do good for others, live a mindful, thoughtful-life God. God was the anchor. God was represented by the community of Sisters, in unison with the Blessed Virgin Mary in her blue robe. It wasn't so much about how Jesus suffered on the cross or even how his sword-pierced heart had dripped blood. It wasn't about God sitting somewhere on a heavenly throne, or even the Holy Spirit as a white dove hovering overhead. It was Mary and this group of Sisters who did good work in the world.

I ached for the closeness I'd felt at Alpha House. Occasional phone calls with Norma weren't enough to fill the gap.

Perhaps that was when I began to loosen my ties to being Sister Maura. Maybe it was picturing Mary doing what she believed God wanted. She had a baby, one they said had been immaculately conceived. I understood that this meant that she never had sex with Joseph. She believed that she could do what God wanted even when it seemed impossible. She got together with Joseph, got pregnant, had baby Jesus. And the rest is history. Or so they said.

I didn't get into the whole question of "what did Joseph think when Mary was pregnant without her having had sex with him?" I just thought she did what God wanted her to do, and Joseph followed along. It was easy back then to believe the stories they told me about God and Jesus and Mary and the Catholic Church as the one, true church. Until then, being Sister Maura and teaching was enough for me.

Until it wasn't.

I was worn down by the changes that had engulfed me. In 1973, when Alpha House closed and I moved into the Aquinas convent, I needed respite. Convents like Aquinas gave the impression of staying in the past with their quiet hallways, private rooms, and chapels devoted to Mass and meditation. My teaching job was a short distance down the walk that connected the convent to the school. Despite this advantage,

I knew it might be difficult for me to adjust. Alpha House had offered a family environment where we talked about our day and supported one another. I loved the feeling of helping others and being valued as a part of the group; it was different from the family I'd grown up in on Olmstead Avenue. There we kept to ourselves and rarely talked about how we were doing.

The majority of the Aquinas Sisters welcomed me. Sister Eileen, a fellow science teacher, invited me to her birthday party; Sister Maureen asked me to join her in the seminar on individualized learning that changed how I taught biology. Some, though, seemed standoffish. My regular clothes stood out among their shortened habits and veils. When I walked past Sister Louisa, she eyed my pink blouse and scowled. Perhaps she saw my contemporary clothing—and me—as a threat to her traditional way of life.

Aquinas was an oasis amidst the densely populated, bustling neighborhood. A constant stream of trucks drove past our doors as they navigated narrow one-way streets to supply stores and restaurants on Arthur Avenue's Little Italy. The school was three stories high and built out of red brick with a tiled roof—a stark contrast to the multi-story apartment buildings around it. Iron gates at the front entrance were locked at night. I wondered if they were locking us in or keeping the neighbors out. The convent had wood paneled walls and a cook who prepared lunch and dinner. My first-floor bedroom had a bathroom that connected to an empty bedroom on the other side. Several months after I moved in, this gave me an idea about how I might help a friend.

Suzanne, who had taken classes with me at Fordham, needed to have back surgery. Her apartment was a fifth-floor walk-up with no elevator, not an option after surgery. She had little money and no family nearby. That's when I remembered the empty bedroom next to mine. Why not ask the Sisters if Suzanne could move in for a few weeks while she recuperated? I had graduated from Fordham University and now took classes toward my Master's degree at Hunter College. I could take care of her in between teaching and going to Hunter. I asked Sister Margaret, the principal, if I could put the question on the agenda for the next convent meeting. When I told her my idea, she said, "Let's discuss it with the other Sisters."

A week later I stood in the convent dining room as a dozen or so Sisters waited for me to begin. "I think that when our community encouraged us to meet the needs of the poor, they had people like Suzanne in mind. She went to Fordham University with me, is single, needs back surgery, and is in dire need for a place to live while she recovers. Her apartment is five flights up with no elevator. I'm asking if we might offer her room and board for a few weeks until she's back on her feet. She could stay in the room next to me. I can bring her meals, which she is willing to pay for, and take care of her until she can walk. Would you be willing to allow her to live with us on a short-term basis?"

Silence filled the room. Sister Louisa shook her head. A few others shifted in their chairs.

Then Sister Eileen spoke up, talking at her usual hyper speed. "I support the idea. Why not help someone in need? We have plenty of room and enough food for everyone." She looked around for support.

All eyes turned to the principal, Sister Margaret. "I hear what you're asking, Sister Maura. It's certainly not something we've done before."

Sister Louisa smirked.

Sister Margaret continued. "But, as Sister Eileen reminded us, we have plenty of room and easy access for someone recovering from surgery." She paused as Sister Louisa's mouth opened in disbelief. "Sister Maura, can you assure us that your friend will stay in her room and not impinge upon the privacy of the Sisters?"

"Absolutely, Sister Margaret."

With that, we took a vote and, with the exception of Sister Louisa, we agreed to allow Suzanne to stay with us.

Suzanne had surgery and moved in. Her windows looked out onto the cloister walk, which filled her room with the scent of honeysuckle and roses. She told me that the sounds of students laughing as they entered and left the building reminded her of her own high school days.

The cook added extra portions to her meals, saying, "Your friend needs good food to heal."

A few weeks later, Suzanne packed her belongings, and I drove her home. I knew that I'd done the right thing even though the divide between Sister Louisa and me persisted. She turned away when I took a seat in the dining room and when she passed in the hall. This added to the discomfort I felt as my career as a teacher entered the next phase.

✧

I LIKED SCIENCE. It followed straightforward rules, ones I could count on. It seemed so simple. Until actual teenage students entered my classroom.

Oh, my, I thought, as my first class of forty-five girls walked into the General Biology classroom. I was certain that "new teacher" was etched on my face as I stood there in a simple blue dress with a Peter Pan collar damp with perspiration.

"Welcome to General Biology. My name is Sister Maura."

The students looked up and waited. They were sophomores, fifteen years old. In spite of their youth, some looked older, wise in ways I wasn't. The sea of navy blazers, white blouses, and gray plaid skirts provided a semblance of order but did little to mask their diversity. Unlike the high school I had attended or the students I'd taught in Saint Brendan's, these faces ranged from white to varying shades of cream, tan, coffee, and ebony. Their hair ran from bleached blonde to Afros and everything in between. Even if I knew the subject material, would I know how to teach such a diverse group of teenage girls?

"Please open your textbook to the first chapter." Could they hear my heart thudding? I was breathing fast as I described how I'd use pop quizzes to test their comprehension. They groaned.

"Give it a chance, ladies. We're in this together."

A few months before school started, I reviewed the teacher's manual. I was relieved to see that the material hadn't changed much since I'd taken the course in high school. Perhaps teaching science wouldn't be as hard as teaching third grade. Then, as the months went by, reality kicked in.

"Isn't it amazing? Plants convert the carbon dioxide we breathe out into the oxygen we breathe in." Even I felt my attention wander as I pointed out the life cycle of a leaf. Many students stared off into space as I continued the lesson. One student stared at me, then out the window. Like the others, she was bored. By the end of the school year, some had to attend summer school to pass the course. I felt like I had let them down. Something had to change. That summer, thanks to Sister Maureen, I took a seminar in how to customize learning for individual students. Was it possible that changing the tools I used to teach biology would enable students to learn more effectively? It took all summer to craft new lesson plans but, by fall, I was ready.

When the next class took their seats, I announced, "Ladies, this course will be different from any other you've taken. You will choose the grade you want. If you successfully complete all the lessons linked to that grade, you will get that grade. If you want an A," I pointed to the handouts in the red box, "you do these assignments. If you want a B . . . ," I pointed to the green box; "or a C . . . ," I pointed to the purple box, "or a D . . . ," I indicated the yellow box. "If you don't complete the assignments, you are choosing to fail and will receive an F."

They looked confused. Several hands shot up.

"Sister, I've never gotten an A. You mean, all I do is complete the assignments and I'll get an A? No way."

They all laughed and shook their heads.

"Yes. You're correct. If you want an A, complete the assignments in the red box and you'll get an A. If you don't complete all the assignments for the grade you chose, I'll grade you on what you do complete."

They looked at me like I was crazy.

It took a few weeks for them to get going, but it worked. The students were thrilled. Some of them told me their parents couldn't believe how well they were doing. As the course went on, they worked hard and passed their mid-term exams with the grades they had signed up for. Many got their first A, others a B, and a few got C. No one failed. I met with Sister Maureen, the history teacher—who'd also changed her teaching method—to compare notes on how our classes were going. My breathing eased. There was hope.

As I walked through the classroom, I saw them turn to help others in their study group, discussing photosynthesis and mitosis as the classroom filled with laughter and conversation. During the last few minutes of each class, quiet descended as they mulled over what they'd learned. I loved watching them spark off each other. I wondered, what if education was always like this? What if teachers taught in more creative ways? What if we had fun while we learned?

I joined with several other teachers who decided to coordinate lessons so they linked together. The inspiration? The United Farm Workers Union had started a grape boycott to protest poor working conditions. We decided to help our students better understand the challenges that farmworkers faced to bring food to us by linking each of our courses with a common theme. I focused on the health effects of pesticides on crops; the religion teacher taught Liberation Theology; the English teacher shared stories about migrant workers around the world; and Sister Maureen traced the history of agricultural labor. We ended our academic collaboration on farmworker issues with a school-wide assembly and a keynote address by Delores Huerta, cochair of the United Farm Workers Union. The auditorium echoed with the student body chanting,

"Si, se puede."

"Yes, we can."

I knew this was what my vocation as a Sister should be about—working together to help others, not just memorizing biological terms. I was catapulted into a world of solidarity. I was pumped and felt more at home in my life as Sister Maura.

TEAM TEACHING ON farmworker issues motivated me to start an extracurricular activity on community organizing. Several teachers hosted after-school clubs that included basketball, knitting, and yearbook—subjects that didn't interest me. What got my attention was how farmworkers and others worked together to make changes. What helped them succeed? I invited Sister Jean from Saint Martin of Tours parish as a guest speaker for my new community organizing activity. Several of my students from General Biology signed up. Sister Jean was involved with the neighborhood association that wanted to improve the living conditions for folks in our neighborhood. Many residents had damaged ceilings, flooded bathrooms, and overflowing sewage. Her parishioners negotiated with landlords, filed complaints with the city, and, as a last resort, staged rent strikes.

One of my students, Elena, spoke up a few months after the last session with Sister Jean. "Sister Maura, I've been thinking a lot about what we learned from the Farm Workers Union and Sister Jean. All of us rent apartments in buildings like the ones that Sister Jean talked about. Here's what I think—how we can improve our *own* lives?"

Everyone turned to her.

"Many of us have problems like the ones Sister Jean talked about. For example, my building had no heat last winter. None. I went to bed wearing my winter clothes to make it through the night. The super said that the owner doesn't have the money to fix the boiler. But we pay rent whether he fixes it or not. It's wrong, Sister."

Elena looked around as the others nodded their support. "We had a meeting with the tenants in my building and sent a letter to the owner saying that we'd take action if he didn't fix the boiler. A lot of people got sick last year when we had no heat. Remember that nasty weather we had? Our apartment was freezing all the time. We complained to the super, the owner, and the city, but no one helped us. So, we took a vote." She looked at me and pointed a finger at the ceiling to emphasize what she was saying. "Like Sister Jean's tenants, instead of paying rent, we're putting the money into a separate bank account until we get what we've asked for. Until then, we're going on a rent strike!"

At this, the others clapped and several whistled their agreement. I was floored. For a moment I couldn't breathe. *Was this my fault?*

Rosa raised her hand, rainbow beads in her dreadlocks swaying as she stood. "Sister, I live in Elena's building. My family and I are with her 100 percent, and so are the other tenants."

I took a long breath, my voice tight. "Girls, I understand why you're doing this, but you're talking about serious issues here. If you withhold rent, your landlord may take action too—maybe even take you to court or evict you and your families." At this, the enthusiasm in the room deflated as if I'd crushed the air out of it.

Then Rhonda stood up, her body pulsating with energy as she raised her hand in a fist. "Sister, I'm committed to helping Rosa and Elena in their fight. And you're right. This *is* serious. Something has to change."

Elena walked over to Rhonda, waved Rosa over, and they linked arms. "We're in this together, Sister. We understand how important this is. These are our homes we're talking about, not just a homework assignment or after-school activity. It has nothing to do with you or the school or Sister Jean. This is us needing a safe place to live."

The rest of the girls gathered around them and they all hugged. I joined them, adding my arms to theirs, offering a prayer to Mary to protect them in their quest.

Several months later, Elena and Rosa's landlord gave in to their demands and fixed the boiler in time for winter. My students had shown me how to fight for what was right.

✧

LATER THAT YEAR, the city decided to close Fordham Hospital, the hospital closest to Aquinas, and the one most of our students used. Even though the city planned to build a new hospital to replace it, it would be farther away and hard to reach by bus.

Elena was mad. "Sister, that's where we brought my brother when he got pneumonia. They can't close it." The rest of the girls chimed in about how their parents worked there or used it for emergencies.

Sister Jean and the neighborhood association invited us to the demonstration to keep the hospital open. My students and I walked down Crotona Avenue with a large crowd that held signs and chanted "Save Our Hospital." People shouted support from the sidewalks and waved to us from apartment windows as we passed by. When we got to the hospital, my students pushed me to the front of the crowd and Sister Jean handed me a megaphone.

"What should I say?"

"Just speak from the heart," Sister Jean whispered as she walked me up the hospital steps.

So, I spoke. "The city doesn't care if our neighborhood loses its hospital. They don't care that the new hospital is three bus rides away or that most of you can't afford an ambulance. We need our hospital. Keep our hospital. Keep our hospital."

The crowd joined in to chant, "Keep our hospital." Blood rushed through my face, my heart opened wider as we chanted and cheered. The city closed the hospital a few months later, but I knew I'd done what I needed to do—I'd combined words with action to tell the truth. In that moment I felt more rooted in my vocation as Sister Maura than ever before.

Ten

TURNING POINTS

IN SPITE OF using the individualized learning approach in my biology class, I was unsure how to energize the other subject I taught—Health Education. One topic in particular worried me—Human Sexuality. What did I know about sex or boyfriends or intimate relationships? Nothing. I could teach the anatomy part, but the students in this class were juniors and seniors. I was a twenty-three-year-old virgin who'd never dated. They had more life experience than I did. Many had boyfriends and were sexually active.

And how did I know that they were sexually active? They told me. These Bronx girls did not hold back.

"You know, Sister," one student said, "when my boyfriend grabs my tits, I slap him. But he just comes back for more."

"Oh, that's nothing," another student chimed in as she wiped chalk from her hands after cleaning the blackboard. "Mine wants me so bad he . . ."

"Girls, hold on. Show respect for yourself by not giving in." They nodded, looked at the floor, and left the classroom.

I bluffed my way through each lesson. I figured that even

if they'd guessed I was naïve, they still needed to pass the class if they wanted to graduate. Each day I put on my I-know-what-I'm-doing face. Each afternoon I went home exhausted and dreading the next class.

A few things happened to change this.

First, Gayle, a senior, came to me after class. She was failing the course because she didn't turn in assignments. "Sister Maura." This was not like her. She never looked up or asked questions. If I asked her a question, she'd shrug and look at her desk.

"Yes, Gayle?"

"Do you have a brother named Peter?"

Oh, no, not Peter. He was my youngest brother who worked as a bartender at an Irish bar in the next neighborhood. She must have met him there. "Yes, I do."

Her eyes flew open and she gasped. "You do?" She took a breath, then added, "Oh. He said to say hello."

"Good," I managed to say.

I called him, my anger spilling over. "Peter, what did you say to Gayle McMaster?"

"Hello, Maura. What happened to starting with 'Hello Peter?' And who's Gayle?"

"She's an Aquinas student you talked to at the bar."

"Maura, she could be anyone. When girls from Aquinas come in, I ask if any of them have Sister Maura. If they say yes, I tell them, 'That's my sister the Sister.' They tell me you're strict, that's all. I think it's kind of cute, don't you—my sister the Sister?"

"Promise me you'll stop talking about me with Aquinas students. I have enough trouble getting them to pay attention in class."

"Okay. But I still like calling you my sister, the Sister."

I hung up the phone. He was my baby brother and meant no harm. Plus, I liked my new nickname—my sister the Sister.

After that Gayle started to do her homework. She even looked up from time to time when I asked a question. In some strange way, having a bartender brother might have helped. Whatever it was, I was relieved that she'd pass the class and graduate.

The second thing that changed was my finding a way to teach about homosexuality, the next topic in the chapter. I decided that even if I didn't have any personal knowledge, I could ask for help. My torturous year teaching third grade had taught me that. But who could I talk to about homosexuality? Then, it dawned on me—it was 1972 and I lived in New York City, a mecca for gays and lesbians. Or so the newspapers said. Gay power was just poking its head out of the closet.

So, I did what we did back then when we needed help. I picked up the phone book. I opened to the *L*'s, scanned down the page, and stopped when I saw what I needed—Lesbian Alliance. They'd know something about homosexuality.

The phone call went like this. "Lesbian Alliance. How may I help you?"

"Hello. This is Sister Maura from Aquinas High School in the Bronx. I'd like to see if your organization can send a guest speaker on homosexuality to my class. Perhaps next week?"

Silence.

"Hello. Is anyone there?"

I heard someone breathing into the phone. In. Out. Then a voice choked out, "Uh. Yes, Sister. Can you hold the line, please?"

A few minutes later a woman picked up the call and we made the arrangements.

The two women who came to my class looked nervous when I met them at the front door. The classroom went quiet when they introduced themselves. They talked about their experience and asked if there were any questions. The girls looked away before one student raised her hand, then another, and another as the room filled with a discussion on homosexuality. When I walked those women out of the building, I thanked them for teaching us more than any textbook could have.

The next day, the principal called me into her office. Her six-foot frame loomed over me as she said, "Sister Maura, several parents called to tell me they were concerned about the presentation by the . . . guest speakers you invited to your Health Education class."

"Oh really? Why is that, Sister?"

She frowned. "Sister Maura, we do not support that lifestyle and . . ."

"Sister Margaret, all I did was ask them to share their experience on a subject you and I knew nothing about. They were very professional."

She shook her head. "In the future, you will get permission from me before you invite any outside speaker to your class."

"Yes, Sister."

I practically skipped down the hall, knowing I was on to something. I decided right then I'd never ask permission to invite guest speakers. I knew that having guest speakers, no matter who they were, wasn't enough to get me thrown out of the school or the convent.

I imagined those two young women as they left the school, shaking their heads at the crucifix on the walls knowing that the Catholic and other churches rejected homosexuals. Maybe they wondered what I was thinking when I invited them?

And what *was* I thinking? That I needed help. And how better to get it than to ask someone who knew more than I did? I followed my instincts and asked for help even when it meant reaching out to people outside my small world. After that I felt lighter, like I had an idea of how to teach this course—by trusting my instincts.

Decades later, I visited the school and saw the former principal. She seemed smaller to me, but her eyes bore into mine when she said, "Maura Doherty. I always wondered what happened to you."

Here was a woman who had dedicated her life to the school's academic program while giving students a safe learning environment. We talked for a few minutes before I left to visit Sister Eileen. I laugh when I think about inviting those gay women to my class. Who would have imagined that quiet Sister Maura would challenge the school's homophobia by asking lesbians to discuss homosexuality?

⟡

MIDWAY THROUGH THE school year, soon after inviting lesbians into my class, the principal called me back into her office. The statue of Our Lady looked on from a shelf behind the desk, her blue robe caught in a shaft of sunlight.

Sister Margaret looked up from papers on her desk.

"Sister, I understand that you're not following the traditional teaching method in your biology class."

"Yes, you're correct. The seminar I took last summer taught me a more effective way to teach. It's going quite well and the students are excelling."

She stood up. "That's all well and good. But here's the curriculum for the exam the students will need to take at the end of the year in addition to the one for general biology." She handed me a sheaf of papers from the New York State Board of Regents that outlined a more intensive course than the General Biology class I was teaching.

She continued. "As you know, doing well on Regents exams will give students a chance at college scholarships."

I looked at the course outline. "Sister, I'm following the general biology curriculum, not the Regents. The students are not prepared for this higher-level exam."

She looked at me, her voice rising. "Sister, I didn't make myself clear. They *will* take the Regents exam in June."

I looked over at Mary, her robe now in shadow as clouds blocked the sun from the window.

"It's not fair to the students to take this on midyear." I paused. "I have another idea. Let's give them the option to take the Regents exam in addition to the general exam, so long as they stay after school to study the new material. The rest of the students can take just the general biology test."

She sighed, "I'll agree to that. But next year, you will follow the Regents curriculum. Is that understood?"

I nodded and left her office, glad that I'd come up with a temporary compromise. But how in the world was I going to do the additional tutoring with my graduate courses and other responsibilities? I'd figure it out. When I gave the students the option, some agreed to study for both exams. We met the following week.

"Girls, this lesson describes the cell, the basic building block of life. Cells join together to form tissues with specialized functions—some are programmed to digest food, like the stomach and intestines, others carry electrical impulses that allow the brain and nervous system to function." My wooden pointer picked out each part on the chart that was mounted on the wall, as if I was selling them a car, showing them all the options inside. "The organelles do most of the work and each one has a special job to do in the body."

Sally squinted at the chart, as she tried to follow along.

"These handouts tell you what pages in your new textbook you'll focus on this week. You'll need to memorize each one. Let's look at the first diagram."

Juanita pointed a finger at the drawing in her book. "Sister, all of this is inside me? Like, right now?"

I nodded as the girls laughed, but Juanita was right. The human body was intricately designed to carry on life. It was a lot to learn, and we had only half the school year to prepare for the final exam.

The general biology class was going well but teaching it and extra study sessions was exhausting. I dreamed about organelles fighting off mitochondria and digestive juices devouring neurons. I'd wake up tangled in sweaty sheets worried that the students would fail their final exams. If that happened, I'd fail as a teacher and a Sister.

At the same time, I began to have doubts about living in the Aquinas convent. Sister Margaret and the other Sisters worked hard and were dedicated to providing quality education to the students. Living with them, however, was different.

At first it felt good to live and work close to school. But now it felt oppressive. The thick brick walls felt like a fortress keeping the neighborhood at bay, the same neighborhood where my students lived and fought for safe living conditions. I had the option, once the motherhouse gave permission, to live where I wanted. When Sister Minnie, formerly Kevin Francis, and two other Sisters invited me to share an apartment with them, I said yes. I hoped it would give me some distance from school and a chance to share community with a smaller group. I packed my suitcase, said goodbye to the Aquinas convent, and made my way to my new apartment, hoping it might feel more like home.

◆

THE MOTHERHOUSE REMINDED me that it had been almost seven years since I'd left the novitiate, and it was time to take final vows. Several of the Sisters I'd entered with had already done so. Every time I thought about spending the rest of my life as Sister Maura, my heart said, *Don't do it*. At the same time my head said, *What? You're thinking of ditching this life after all you went through to get here?* A war raged inside me as I taught school, tutored, conducted after-school activities, and took graduate classes. I was a walking conundrum—calm Sister Maura on the outside but scared Maura on the inside. Everything pushed down on me.

What should I do?

◆

THE METAL SCREEN between Aunt Jo and me divided our worlds. It was a barrier, one that ensured her privacy and kept the secrets and sacredness of the cloister inside. I could only see her through openings in the metal, her face crosshatched with steel. When I was young, words shared between Mom and Aunt Jo moved through this screen and, in later years, between my aunt and me.

The changes brought on by Vatican II had impacted Aunt Jo as well. Cousin John, a Maryknoll priest and Aunt Jo's nephew, had visited her several times post-Vatican II. Mom and I joined him on one of his visits to see her. He wore a pair of slacks and long-sleeved shirt. Mom had on a going-to-church dress, a strand of pearls and matching earrings. I wore a navy blue skirt and white blouse. We entered the familiar parlor with the beige stucco walls, hardback chairs, and overhead light that cast a soft glow. We stood when we heard faint footsteps from behind the wooden shutters that covered the metal screen. When the shutters opened there was Aunt Jo in her brown wool habit and black veil, smiling at us. We gazed at this woman radiant in the mystery of the monastery.

John spoke first. "Aunt Jo, it's time. We've talked about this."

Time for what?

She shook her head.

John looked at her. "Yes, Aunt Jo. It's time."

Her eyes widened.

Was she pleading with him? About what?

She took a step forward, reached up, slid back a bolt, and opened the screen that protected her from us. The hinges gave a soft protest as the screen opened. Mom gasped. I took a step back. How could this be? John stepped up, held out his arms and Aunt Jo moved toward him, their eyes locked before he hugged her. He hugged her! Tears flowed down my face as I watched and turned to Mom whose tears matched mine. John stood back and said, "Tata," his nickname for my mother, and reached for Mom's hand. She took one step, then another, closer and closer to the now open window. She leaned in to hug her sister for the first time in decades. They both cried.

Then I stepped up and hugged her—the nun who had been the untouchable, who lived behind monastery walls and a metal screen. The scratchy brown wool of her habit felt like velvet in that magical moment when my aunt was no longer a mirage but a real, living person.

The sliding back of that bolt, the metal screen swinging open, changed my life. Perhaps that's what cracked my foundation as Sister Maura. Perhaps the certainty that Aunt Jo was inaccessible had held me up, reassured me that I could believe that some things were sacred and beyond change. Yes, I gained so much when I hugged my aunt for the first time and many times after that. But I lost something precious too.

Before this, my life as Sister Maura was something I could count on. I trundled down the track of religious life, teaching, taking graduate classes at Hunter College, then spending weekends at the motherhouse for community council meetings. Day after day, week after week, month after month, year after year, I knew who I was, and where I was headed.

After that screen opened, I wasn't sure anymore.

SHIFTS WERE HAPPENING all around me. We elected Sisters to a new Community Council to make decisions about the future of our community. I'd been elected to the council soon after I'd taken temporary vows and was new to the consensus process. Our meetings were fraught with intense discussion.

Every member had to agree to each decision. As a group we decided where Sisters could live and work and how to spend the money they earned out in the world. Vatican II encouraged religious Sisters to leave behind autocratic positions like Mother Generals and top-down forms of government for more inclusive, democratic systems. Now Sisters voted for council members and an executive team that included a president. In 1971, the question posed to us on the council was how we might use our resources to help the people who lived in neighboring Rockland County. What were the biggest needs? Sisters Ursula and Marie Jean asked that we explore serving seniors who needed housing and supportive care. At first the more conservative Sisters on the council disagreed.

"We are not a social services agency. We are a teaching order and know nothing about housing the elderly. We have our own Sisters to care for and schools to support."

Months later we reached a consensus, and a committee was selected to develop an action plan. As a result, one of the first senior housing developments sponsored by religious Sisters in Rockland County was built on the grounds of the motherhouse. Years later, independent, assisted living, and memory care options emerged as one of the biggest needs in that county and the country. Our community was willing to expand their vision thanks to the foresight of its leaders and the encouragement of Pope John XXIII and Vatican II.

BACK AT AQUINAS High School, my students told me about abusive parents, the need for parents to work multiple jobs to pay bills, their poor housing conditions, and other issues. I didn't know how to help them. The income I earned as a teacher was sent to the motherhouse after bills were paid. I had no worries about where my next meal would come from. My students didn't have that luxury.

When I started the community organizing club, I got a close-up look at what my students and neighbors were facing. Sister Jean showed slides of collapsed ceilings, broken pipes, falling plaster. "This is what our neighbors deal with every day."

My parents owned our duplex on Olmstead Avenue. We always had heat, hot water, and safe living conditions. The problems Sister Jean described shocked me. I realized how little I knew about the reality around me.

On Saturdays I taught Bible studies at Santa Agonia parish in East Harlem. I passed out holy cards and told stories of saints and martyrs to children eager to catapult themselves outside to play with friends. Parents were grateful for my work, but I felt disconnected. What did it matter if they knew that Saint Barbara was beheaded for protecting her faith? Or that Saint Francis of Assisi bore the stigmata, the wounds on his hands and feet similar to those of the crucified Jesus? I began to question what I was doing and how I was living my life.

◇

BEING SISTER MAURA had worked for almost a decade until I realized that I didn't want to do it anymore. I couldn't force myself to take final vows, to commit the rest of my life to being a Sister—even when I pictured Mary in her beautiful blue robe or played the theme song for *Jonathan Livingston Seagull* in my biology class while we examined bird feathers under magnifying glasses. I explained the wonder of barbs and barbules that allowed for the gift of flight. That wonder was not enough to save me from agonizing over my life.

My prayer book from those days, the Saint Joseph Missal from 1966, is filled with mementos—a memorial card for my father, holy cards made by Aunt Jo, and even some I made when I was in the novitiate. One that I made for Mom on Mother's Day shows Mary with her arms around baby Jesus. Father McManus had preached to us in Saint Agnes Chapel from the pulpit high above our heads, as if only he knew what was best. No one could celebrate Mass without a male priest. Why did men have the power over how Sisters celebrated Mass? I joined a group of Sisters at a retreat center owned by the community in upstate New York. We planned our own liturgies and choreographed dance and music to celebrate our Sisterhood and connection to the divine. I felt free, happy, connected to the spirit that we all shared as Sisters and as women. This made sense to me—this connection with my Sisters and the God we served.

I thought of all the Sisters who were doing good in the world, living lives of service. And I thought of Aunt Jo, Mom, and all of us who followed the traditions of the church, going to Mass, praying the rosary. One card contains the prayer, "The Memorare," which means, "Remember."

> Remember, O most gracious Virgin Mary, that never was it known that anyone who fled to thy protection, implored thy help, and sought thy intercession was left unaided. Inspired by this confidence, I fly unto thee, O Virgin of virgins, my mother! To thee do I come, before thee I stand, sinful and sorrowful. O Mother of the Word Incarnate, despise not my petitions, but, in thy mercy, hear and answer me. Amen."

The words "sinful and sorrowful" stopped me. I wasn't sinful and sorrowful. I was a loving, caring woman who helped others. But, underneath all that caring, I was angry, frustrated, and unhappy. I took care of others and ignored my own needs. I didn't know I even had needs.

While I anguished over taking final vows, I visited Cousin John, the Maryknoll priest. We sat in leather chairs in his study on the Marymount campus in the Bronx. Sunlight flooded through beveled windows casting a warm glow across the room.

He poured me something to drink and said, "Maura, I've been meaning to ask you. What do you do for fun?"

My head buzzed. *Fun? I don't have fun. All I do is teach, go to graduate school, and teach some more. There's no room for fun. Nothing is fun.*

Then the truth dawned on me. *Is that why I'm so tired? Because I don't have any fun?*

I made up something like, "Well, last week Sister Lillian played guitar and we sang along."

He nodded and changed the subject. The lie swirled around me as we talked. Yes, we sang, but it wasn't "fun." It was part of the Holy Week services we celebrated before Easter. I used to have fun, didn't I? On the bus ride home I stared out the window. How could I lie to him? How could I lie to myself? I was exhausted. The knot in my throat from denying the desperation I felt threatened to choke me. My neck and shoulders were locked in spasms so tight it was like being trapped in a vise. I couldn't move my neck and I turned my whole body when I needed to look left or right. I wasn't at home in my own body.

Why wasn't I having fun? Wasn't I happy? The brutal

sameness of everyday I spent as Sister Maura, the anxiety of holding it all together, teaching, going to graduate school, acting as confidante to so many of students whose secrets weighed me down, how waving goodbye to so many Sisters who'd left hurt me to the core—Mary Doreen, Beatrice Anthony, Ann McGuire and Anne Marie Cotter from Alpha House, and so many others. How I had sutured my broken heart with staples that never healed so I could push through the work and the stress with a smile on my face.

No one knew the extent of my heartbreak. Not even me.

Until Cousin John asked me what I did for fun, and I couldn't think of anything.

What did I do after that? I prayed harder, studied more, taught lesson after lesson about mitosis and martyrs and told no one what I was feeling—how un-fun my life was, how the thought of taking "final vows" repulsed me, how I hated my life, how I loved my Sister friends and students but hated who I'd become. I'd never heard of counseling and had no spiritual counselor. It wasn't part of my life.

What happened over the next year as I examined my life and found it lacking? I cracked. In those days I knew nothing about therapy. All I could do was pray and figure this out on my own.

And I could do that.

Couldn't I?

When I thought about leaving the convent, I panicked. *Do I want to be Sister Maura for the rest of my life?* When the answer to the question felt like *No*, I fought it. *Who would I be if I left?* I resisted my inner voice. I hunkered down, barely got through each day, the shell of me showing up, going through the motions.

The bolt had unlocked the screen that had kept me intact, and I cracked open.

I didn't know what to do until Mrs. Wojtow spoke to me from her coffin.

eleven

FROM THE COFFIN

THE RAVAGES OF surgery showed on Mrs. Wojtow's face as I knelt on the prie-dieu beside her open casket. It was 1976. Large votive candles flickered on either side of the coffin and threw eerie shadows against the wall. My friend Ellen stood behind me, leaning against her father as they grieved their loss.

That was when I heard Mrs. Wojtow, clear as a bell. "You horse's ass. What are you waiting for?"

Mrs. Wojtow had never minced words. A tough Polish woman who favored perogies and Pall Malls, she'd sit in a haze of cigarette smoke in the kitchen a few feet away as Ellen and I did our homework. She was the only mother I knew who talked irreverently.

"You horse's ass, whatcha doin', girls? Why all the talking in there?"

Ellen would roll her eyes and call out, "Ma, we have a science project. We'll get this done, then take a break."

A break consisted of perogies, stuffed cabbage rolls, kielbasa, and other dishes I'd never eaten before. Nothing like the Velveeta cheese and Ritz crackers served at home.

I got used to how Mrs. Wojtow talked, certainly not like any mother I knew, not mine and not anyone else's. I loved spending time with her and got used to how she talked, She showed love through her food and her snippy comments. I loved how she called out to us, making sure we were doing okay. I felt seen. And wanted. Her death from throat cancer resulted in the woman in the casket not looking anything like the person I'd known.

But the voice was hers.

I got the message. I didn't wonder, was that really her? Why was I hearing from a dead person?

Instead, I thought, what *was* I waiting for? In that instant I said No to the convent and Yes to leaving it. I stood up, said goodbye to Ellen and her father, went back to the apartment and called the motherhouse. I asked Sister Marie Jean, the president of the community, if we could meet the following day. I didn't tell her why I wanted to see her. I wanted to do it in person.

"Tomorrow? How's four o'clock?"

"Yes." If I borrowed a car and left during my free period, I could make it in time.

Sister Gerry lent me her Datsun hatchback which smelled like her latest parish potluck. The aroma of chicken curry wafted around me as I rolled down the window to quell my roiling stomach. Afternoon sun glinted off bare branches on trees along the Sprain Brook Parkway. Would this be my last trip to the motherhouse? I had been a Sister for nine years. Was this the end?

It seemed a lifetime ago that Sister Marie Jean had given me permission to live in Alpha House and to finish my bachelor's degree at Fordham. In fact, she had asked, "Why Fordham? Why not go to Berkeley?"

I think she meant it. Since Fordham was run by Catholic priests, in this case, the Jesuits, she must have suspected it might be limiting for me. And now I couldn't help but wonder how things would have turned out differently if I had gone to California instead of staying in the Bronx. My heart hurt thinking about it. Pain seized my neck as I turned my head to pull ahead of a car in the next lane. Preparing to cut ties with my community and with my commitment to being Sister Maura sent spasms down my shoulders. But I knew I had to do this. My body was commanding me to end the pain of indecision. It was time. My head pounded as I pulled into the parking lot, stepped out, and locked the car. I looked to the left at the novitiate where I'd spent my first two years. Good memories? *Stop thinking about the good. I need permission to leave so I can get on with my life.* No matter how much pain I was in, it would only get worse if I stayed.

A stiff wind pushed me up the steps and through the front door. In front of me was the refectory where I had served countless meals; to the right was the corridor to the elevator that led up to the leadership suite. That's where Sister said to meet her. The hallway was vacant, as if everyone knew this was a solemn moment, this leaving, this signing of final papers. I got off the elevator on the fourth floor and walked into the reception area outside Sister's office. The door to the office was closed. I knocked. No answer. I sat in one of the green upholstered chairs facing the floor to ceiling windows. Our four o'clock appointment time came and went. Then 4:15. And 4:30. I waited until 5:00 p.m. Sister Mary O'Toole walked off the elevator. Her auburn hair fell in curly waves around her face.

"Sister Maura, hello. Who are you waiting for?"

"Sister Marie Jean. She told me to be here at four o'clock."

She shook her head. "I think Sister said she'd be out until late this evening."

I stood up and let out a long breath. There was nothing left to say. I had done everything possible to honor my vocation as a Sister. Sister Marie Jean didn't have the decency to call me to reschedule our appointment. As the elevator doors closed on me, I sagged against the wall. *That's it. I'm done.*

But I wasn't done, was I? There were two and a half months before the end of the school year. It never entered my mind to quit teaching before June. I exited the lobby, unlocked the car, sat down behind the wheel, and sobbed. I cried for me, for the despair I felt, angry at the Sister who represented our community as its leader. How could she treat me like this? I grabbed a crumpled napkin from the passenger seat and wiped my eyes. Now I, too, smelled like leftover curry. I started the car and pulled out. No more tears. Pain, yes. But no more tears.

The next evening Sister Marie Jean called.

"Sister, I understand you were waiting for me yesterday."

My throat closed. "You said we'd meet at four o'clock."

"I think you're mistaken, Sister Maura. I said our meeting was tentative."

Tentative? Why would I drive two hours round trip to the motherhouse if she had said the appointment was tentative?

I steeled myself. "Sister Marie Jean, I've decided to leave the community."

"So I heard. I'm sorry about that."

Then, silence. I tried to make sense of what had just happened. Is that why she hadn't met me? She must have heard about me leaving from rumors around the community. Hadn't it been worth her time to have a final conversation? The buzz in my ears blocked out everything before I said, "Goodbye," and hung up.

A flush of shame and anger raced through me. Spasms shot through my neck and shoulders as I shut the door to my bedroom and lay down.

How was I going to make it until school ended in June?

Looking back, I wonder if I was so distressed about leaving the convent that I hadn't heard her say our appointment was tentative. Or maybe it wasn't that at all. Perhaps Sister Marie Jean had been pummeled by the constant departure of Sisters. She had said goodbye to dozens of close friends and hundreds of others in the wake of the changes after Vatican II. Not showing up for our appointment might have been a sign of how burned out she was. How much she had lost. I was just one of five hundred Sisters who left between 1970 and 1976. That didn't lessen the pain of her not showing up, but it helped me understand why.

✧

IN MAY, 1976 I woke up rigid in pain on Mother's Day. It was as if every muscle pinned me to the bed. Each time I tried to move, I yelped. My roommate Minnie came in to see what was wrong.

"Minnie, I can't move. Help me sit up."

She leaned in, lifted me into a sitting position, and swung my legs around while I groaned. She helped me change out of my pajamas while tears flowed down my cheeks.

"I need to call my mother. She expects me to come see her." I held on to the wall as I inched my way to the phone. When she answered, I said, "Mom, it looks like I'll be late for dinner today. I'm going to ask Minnie to bring me to the emergency room to get help with some muscle pain I'm having. I'll be home after that."

"All right, Maura. I'll see you when you get here."

I hung up and asked, "Minnie, can you drive me to the emergency room? I think I need to get checked out."

She went to get her car keys as I walked into the kitchen where our roommates Gerry and Vera were eating breakfast.

"I'm not sure why my muscles are so tight," I said. "But I'm in a lot of pain. Minnie's going to take me to the emergency room to see if I can get some help."

Gerry said, "Sorry to hear that, Maura."

Vera stood and waved her hands in frustration. "Maura, you know what's happening. You teach health education and know about psychosomatic conditions. You're stressed out." She shook her head and left the kitchen.

Psychosomatic muscle spasms?

Minnie helped me into the car as I turned Vera's words over in my head. Was my body taking on the pain I'd been feeling about the leaving the convent? I didn't know. All I knew was I was in pain, and now I felt like a failure by not knowing my spasms were caused by stress.

The doctor listened to my symptoms, left, and came back with a dixie cup filled with ice. He handed it to me and said, "Rub this on your neck. There's not much more we can do for you."

When I told Minnie what the doctor had said, we both laughed.

"I guess I'd better get some cups of ice stored away in case this happens again." Despite the laughter, despair weighed me down. I had no idea how I would get through the next few days, let alone the next few months. Who would I be if I wasn't Sister Maura?

Minnie and I didn't talk about what Vera had said. Even though she might have been right, I knew that I needed to hang on until the end of the school year and see what would come next.

Harold Tannenbaum was next. As my graduate school advisor, I needed his signature to withdraw from the program, just three credits short of a master's degree in education from Hunter College. With no job prospects, no money to my name, and my body racked in pain, I couldn't see any option aside from dropping out of graduate school. At this point I could barely raise my arms with the pain in my shoulders. I felt imprisoned in my body as if some outside force had taken it over.

"Dr. Tannenbaum. I need to withdraw from the program. Could you sign this, please?"

He looked at the paper I handed him and frowned. "I don't understand, Sister. You are leaving before you finish your degree? Tell me why?"

How could I explain my desperation, how hopeless I felt, how I was leaving the convent in an attempt to save my sanity? How I had no money, no job, no idea of how to take care of myself after I left the convent. He picked up the paper and stared at me, waiting for an answer.

I squeaked out, "Please."

He grabbed a pen, signed the paper, and held it out. "You are a crazy woman, Sister. A crazy woman."

He was right. I was crazy, off my rocker, bereft, besieged. I had no idea what to do except to leave everything behind and find a new life. I took the paper, dropped it at the Registrar's office, and left.

When I told my mother I was leaving the convent, she said, "Why would you leave now? I like your friends."

"I like my friends too, Mom. They're great. But that's not enough reason for me to stay. I'm not happy."

She shook her head and took another puff of her cigarette.

A few days after school ended, the Sister in charge of finances called and asked, "How much money do you think you need?"

How did *I* know how much money I'd need? I'd been in the convent for nine years. My teaching salary was sent to the motherhouse. I'd never rented an apartment or paid bills. Other Sisters did that. I hadn't even known that the motherhouse gave Sisters who left the community severance pay for their years of service. But my leaving had nothing to do with money. I was in deep grief over the loss of my vocation.

All my frustration bubbled up. The pain in my shoulders and necked spiked as I told her, "I don't need your money," and hung up the phone.

A few months later they sent me a check for $3,000. I needed to ask my mother to cash it since I didn't have a bank account. But that wasn't why I was mad. Almost all the Sisters, except for a few friends, ignored me during those final months. I imagine they were burned out from everyone who'd left since Vatican II and were too sad to offer me support. They had turned away from me as I struggled with one of the hardest decisions of my life. Maybe I was also mad at God who wasn't there for me like I thought he'd be.

Perhaps I was mad at myself for spending almost a decade of my life following a dream of being Sister Maura, of having close Sister friends, thinking I was doing the right thing with my life. That dream had disintegrated. I packed my familiar black suitcase, moved in with Mary Byrne, the former Sister Mary Doreen. At night I slept on her couch, then spent every day looking for work, applying for jobs in project management and office support. I steered clear of teaching and anything linked to the Catholic Church. I stopped going to Mass or believing in anything Catholic. Jobs were scarce since the city had declared bankruptcy. As the summer came to an end, my muscles remained clenched in spasms with no job offers in sight.

I never considered moving back home to Olmstead Avenue. My mother lived on Social Security. I refused to ask her to support me. I was twenty-seven years old.

My friend Suzanne, the woman who had lived with me at the Aquinas convent as she recovered from back surgery, came to the rescue. She had recently moved to Washington, DC.

"Why not move to DC? You can stay with me until you find work and your own place to live."

After weeks of sleeping on Mary's couch, I'd had enough. I looked up the schedule for Amtrak trains from Manhattan to DC, said goodbye to friends and family, packed my suitcase, and got on a train south. Sleeping on a couch at Suzanne's felt like a better option. I'd be in a new town where I could reinvent myself without worrying about running into the Sisters I'd left behind.

I started a new life but it had its problems. I was worn down by ongoing spasms in my neck and by the void left after leaving my community. I bought a book on yoga and started to reclaim my body. As I sat on the floor of my studio apartment, I tried to relax like the book said, rolling shoulders one way, then the other, wondering how long it would take me to recover. As I moved through the stretches, a cacophony of howling monkeys and roaring lions echoed from the National Zoo behind my new apartment.

They seemed to share my pain.

◆

I LEFT EVERYTHING Catholic behind. That was in my past. Day by day, I worked to reclaim myself. I lived one day at a time with no thought of a forever future. Yes, I hurt and missed the friendships I had forged in the convent. But there was no going back. I needed to heal and find out who I was. Who I wanted to be. I trusted myself to find my way in this new life. I promised myself to listen to my inner spirit every step of the way.

photographs

First Holy Communion, 1957

(left) Maura; Sister Catherine Mary, middle;
(right) Kathleen Gallagher

Visit to the Motherhouse, Spring 1967

Entrance Day, August 1967

(left to right) brothers Peter and Michael; Maura; Mom; brother John; sisters Colleen and Jo Anne; brother Francis; Dad

Entrance Day, August 1967

(left to right) Mom, Maura, Dad, Sister Beatrice Anthony (B.A.)

Entrance Day, August 1967

Maura going up the steps of the Novitiate

Entrance Day, August 1967
Postulant Sister Kathleen Maura in her new outfit

Entrance Day, August 1967

Sister Kathleen Maura with family and friends.
(*middle*) Sister Beatrice Anthony (B.A.).

Postulant Band, 1967

Sister Margaret Gerard in white habit;
(back row to her left) Sister Kathleen Maura

Postulant Sister Kathleen Maura, 1967

Novice Sister Kathleen Maura, 1968

(left) sister Jo Anne; *(right)* sister Colleen

Novices Sister Kathleen Maura and Mary Doreen, 1968

Sister Maura's Temporary Vows, 1969

(left) Sister Beatrice Anthony; *(right)* Sister Kathleen Maura

part three

After

CELTIC SPIRAL
THE WILL TO MOVE FORWARD
AND OVERCOME ADVERSITY

Twelve

FIRST BOYFRIEND

MY FIRST JOB after leaving the convent and moving to DC was working at a nonprofit organization called Maryland Action. I was twenty-seven and felt adrift amidst the dozen new hires who sat around me. They looked like they were nineteen or twenty years old. Was I really the oldest one there? Fortunately, the staff person ready to give a fifteen-minute update before we started our shift looked about ten years older than me.

"Welcome, everyone," said the slightly pudgy man at the front of the room. "I'm Barry Greever, lead researcher for Maryland Action. I'm here to show you why your work is so crucial. As you may know, we're focusing your door-to-door canvassing in the town of Chevy Chase. Our goal is to raise money so we can lobby the legislature for a citizens' utility board. A CUB. It would have a say in setting the rates charged for gas, water, and electric bills." As he turned to pick up a yardstick to point to statistics written on the board, a young man beside me turned to me and sighed. "Pretty boring, huh? Want to go for a beer after work?" I shook my head.

Barry continued. "The median income for voters in Chevy Chase is higher than in other parts of the state. Being so close to the District of Columbia means many high-level government officials live there. The folks in Chevy Chase pay a lot for utility bills and might be willing to donate to our cause. In the phone surveys we've conducted over the past few months, the majority of them think their bills are too high. That's why you'll be canvassing."

I raised my hand.

He looked at me. "Ask away. No need to raise hands."

My face flushed hot. My Catholic school training had kicked in. "Why canvass? Why not ask them over the phone if they'll donate? Why not get a commitment for the money right then instead of having to go door-to-door?"

He nodded. "Okay, everyone. What do you think? Remember, all questions, all ideas are on the table until we decide as a group if another idea is better."

Belinda, who was on a gap year from American University, spoke up. "Phone calls lack the immediacy of a face-to-face conversation. That's the advantage of canvassing folks one-on-one."

"Okay. How many agree with Belinda?

Several folks agreed.

"Who'd vote to go with phone calls to get donations? A few did. "Now, let's see which idea works best. We tried both approaches last year. Here's what happened." He grabbed what look like a stack of oversized punch cards and a knitting needle. "Look at our results." He held up a stack of cards. "These cards have info on all the voters in Chevy Chase." He stuck the needle in a hole in the three-inch stack of cards. "During the phone survey, these folks supported a CUB and said they'd donate to help get it started." A quarter of the cards fell into his other hand. "Here's how many actually donated after a follow up phone call." He put the needle in again and counted out seven cards. "Out of hundreds of folks who said they'd give us money, only seven did."

In 1976, a time before the internet, before Excel spreadsheets and cell phones, Barry had created another way of evaluating data. He seemed modest, yet also sure of himself. Then he held out a different stack of cards for over a hundred other people.

"Belinda is correct. When we canvassed voters directly, we brought in over a hundred donations ranging from $5 to $100. That's why we're sending you into other neighborhoods to help create a CUB. You're the backbone of this effort. We can't do this work without you. Questions?"

I was impressed. Maybe Barry was onto something, even though knocking on strangers' doors was out of character for me, a Bronxite.

A few weeks later, Barry came to me after a staff meeting. "It's Maura, right? How's it going?"

"I'm getting the hang of it," I said. "Your demonstration with the cards was impressive."

"Thanks. They've been a great tool for a lot of communities around the South. I'd love to tell you more. Why don't you come to the annual meeting next Saturday? I'm going to tell folks how my research is helping us as well as supporting miners in Appalachia."

"I might just do that." I was intrigued. Barry had experience with good work here and around Appalachia, a place I knew nothing about. I decided to go to the meeting to learn more.

⋄

ON SATURDAY, I took a seat at the back of the room and waved to Belinda at the end of the row. She moved to the chair next to me.

"Can't get enough, huh?" As she spoke, a mass of tight red ringlets that were gathered on the top of her head bobbed in unison.

I laughed. "I want to hear more about what Barry's doing. I'm glad canvassing helps the organization, but I think there's a whole lot more to the story." Maybe Barry's next talk would motivate me to keep this job until I found something better.

At the front of the room, Barry sorted cards to show our progress raising money. After answering a few questions, he explained how using the card system and what he called "participatory research" was helping other groups, including coal miners on strike in Kentucky.

"We think we're up against some challenges here in Maryland. These miners are being harassed by hired goons and put in jail. All the miners want is safe working conditions. The same kind of research we use here helped them prove that the judge who jailed them was crooked. He was removed and the miners were released. Showing folks how to use the power of information is key."

I started to imagine what it would have been like if Barry had supported my Bronx students as they fought for safe housing. That would have been quite a match.

He picked up a guitar and strummed a few chords. "A little bit of music sure helps us along, don't you agree?" Within minutes he had the audience singing "Gonna Go to Work on Monday, One More Time," and ending with a resounding "We Shall Overcome." I felt more energized than I had in a long while. Canvassing door to door wasn't inspiring me. But this was. Barry was into something important, and the songs of liberation were written for people in real need, not just folks wanting to lower utility bills.

Barry invited me to coffee a few times. It turned out that he lived in my apartment building, just a few floors above me. The more we talked, the more I liked him. His dedication to fight for those in need resonated with me. Even though he was from rural Virginia and I was from the Bronx, we both wanted to help others. He wasn't good looking, but he radiated good energy. I loved spending time with him. As we got to know each other, I felt more and more attracted to him. Me, the former Sister Maura, had met my first boyfriend.

One night as we hugged and kissed, he asked me what I liked when I made love. Me? I had no idea what I liked. I had no idea how to make love.

"Don't worry, Maura. We can take it slow. Just holding you and kissing you feels so good." Barry snuggled next to me and sighed.

WE TOOK A road trip that included camping in the Blue Ridge Mountains with a visit to his friends in Virginia and Tennessee. I'd only camped once before but he reassured me that he had everything we needed. Meeting his friends in Appalachia would be a plus. His orange Karman Ghia fit all our gear and purred down the road. I didn't expect the vibrant red foliage around our campsite. We cooked hot dogs and beans over an open fire and listened as owls called overhead.

As the campfire danced and sparked, he pulled out his guitar and strummed a tune.

"Have you heard this one? 'There once was a union maid who never was afraid . . .'"

As he sang, I felt his passion. My heart opened. Here was a kindred spirit who wanted to make things better and teach others how to do it. That night, when we made love, I felt loved and cared for.

The next morning the trees were covered in a dusting of snow, as if another miracle had occurred in the night. I took it all in. Such beauty. Such love surrounded me.

AFTER WE DROVE into Tennessee he said, "I want you to meet some people." He pulled down a gravel road that wound past round buildings and a large garden. "This is Highlander Center." He smiled, his red mustache curling upwards as he continued. "I helped them find out how mining companies were robbing people of their land and mineral rights. Coal is money in Appalachia."

That afternoon I listened as Barry, John Gaventa, and Juliet Merrifield, traded stories about the greed of coal companies and the floods that ravaged land decimated by strip mining.

John looked at Barry. "We dug deeper into Peabody Coal Company's holdings. You and I were right. The company has stolen mineral rights from more folks than we had imagined. Folks own their homes but not the coal under them."

Barry grunted, his shoulders sagged, "What's your plan?"

As they talked about next steps, I glanced at a pamphlet that summarized Highlander's history. Since the 1940s, it had been at the center of the civil rights movement. Rosa

Parks had attended an organizing session there before she sat down in the front of the bus defying the edict that Blacks only sit in the back.

When I looked up, Juliet was filling Barry in on their work with coal miners. "Helen Lewis wrote a grant that allowed Appalachian and Welsh miners to visit each other. Amazing work. Sure enough, they found out they were all fighting a common enemy—greedy owners who bypassed safety to mine coal. The cases of black lung in both groups are astounding. The miners are suffocating from coal dust and risking their lives every day they go to work."

As they talked, I felt overwhelmed. I knew nothing about coal miners, except the little Barry had talked about. My past as a high school teacher and canvasser paled in comparison to the work they were doing. Demonstrating to protest the closing of Fordham Hospital came nowhere near the battle these folks were waging.

When Juliet turned to me and asked what kind of I work I'd been doing, I mumbled, "I taught high school science and helped students fight greedy landlords." Then, my brain froze. It was as if I had to process everything I was hearing before I could say anything more. As Barry and I drove away from Highlander, I had a feeling this experience would stay with me. I promised myself that somehow, sometime, I would return to Highlander and know what to say.

Thirteen

WORK

EVEN THOUGH I had gotten used to canvassing, a minimum wage of $2.30 an hour barely paid the rent. And I had another goal in mind. I wanted to go to Ireland to meet my relatives. Mom rarely talked about them, but I knew that both she and Dad had family there. After working for a year as a canvasser, I got a job as a sales rep for Ayerst Labs, a pharmaceutical company. Working for a corporation didn't appeal to me, but the money I made would allow me to get to Ireland. I had no trouble getting most of the physicians to listen for a few minutes while I told them about the latest heart medication or popular anesthetic gas. Some refused to see me, but thanks to my previous job, I expected that. I easily met my quota to see a certain number of physicians a day.

But within a few months I knew something had to change. I was bored. Talking about medications wasn't enough. It was one thing to leave the convent where I helped others, but it was another thing to drive a white Ford LTD with a trunk full of sample medications all over DC and Maryland. I wanted to save money for my Irish trip, but how could I keep a job that wasn't challenging me?

DR. BRESETTE'S OFFICE in Georgetown smelled of lemon Pledge, its side tables gleaming the way they did back home on Olmstead Avenue. When I spotted a food donation box with a flyer for the Zacchaeus Free Clinic, something clicked.

The receptionist handed me back my business card with her verdict, "The doctor does not see sales reps."

I leaned in and lowered my voice. "I want to hear about the clinic." We locked eyes and she scanned me like Wonder Woman to see if I was telling the truth. After a few seconds she picked up the phone.

Within a few minutes the doctor stood in the doorway and called me over. Patients in the waiting room put down their magazines and stared. I'm sure they wondered how I'd managed to see the doctor before them. He was taller than me, with curly black hair. He reminded me of a stallion that had just raced around the track. I had only a few seconds to get what I needed.

"Doctor, I want to know about the clinic." I motioned to the flyer on the wall. "I'd like to volunteer. I'm from the Bronx, was in the convent for nine years, and taught in a low-income neighborhood. I think I might be able to help."

Brown eyes seared into mine before he spoke. "We do need volunteers. Meet me there Saturday morning at nine o'clock. Judy," he pointed to the receptionist, "will get you the address." He turned and closed the door behind him.

Judy grabbed a pen, sniffed at me, and handed me the information.

I felt lighter when I left his office. When I got back to my apartment, I invited Barry to join me on Saturday. Even if I wasn't sure how to help them, Barry, the prized researcher, might have an idea and, between the two of us, we'd figure something out.

CONCRETE STEPS THAT sloped in the middle led to the entrance of the clinic in a house off Logan Circle. Lights in the entryway highlighted peeling wallpaper and scuffed linoleum floors. A woman named Rachelle went to find Dr. Bresette, and Barry and I settled on a plaid couch pocked with cigarette holes and smelling of mildew. The air reeked of smoke and car exhaust from the open door. *What have I gotten myself into?* Then the doctor came in, gave us a warm smile, and shook our hands. It took just a minute for him to show us the clinic, since it consisted of two small exam rooms off the narrow hall.

"Doctor Bresette..."

"We go by first names here, Maura. It's how we break down barriers for the people we serve."

"John?"

"Make it Jack and I promise I'll answer you."

"Okay, Jack. Tell us what you could use most."

"We serve patients who have nowhere else to go. The clinic runs entirely on donations. We could use help getting our clients on Medicaid." He shook his head. "Our care is free, but we only offer limited services. Most of our folks need additional treatment they can't afford. They haven't applied for Medicaid and don't realize they might even qualify for it."

Barry asked him a few questions about how the clinic kept its records. Jack told him they were stored in a file cabinet. In 1977, hard copies were the only option for keeping patient information. We promised to return the following Saturday.

On our next visit I told Jack, "We think we can help you

with two things. I'll help your clients sign up for Medicaid. And Barry has an idea he'd like to tell you about." I knew nothing about Medicaid, but thought I could figure it out. Since I'd managed classrooms of energetic teenagers, I assumed I could divine the intricacies of a federal program.

Barry reached into his pocket and pulled out a stack of familiar-looking punch cards. "Jack, you mentioned that the clinic applies for grants. I think I might be able to help you summarize information on your clients to make that easier. Here's a system I set up for the nonprofit I work for." He went on to explain how the cards worked and demonstrated how they were used to find out who had signed up to donate money or to volunteer. "If I set up cards for your clients, I could enter their personal information, male, female, street address, and the services they've received. Then you could sort the cards according to which services your clients received as well as their demographics."

Jack leaned in. "That's intriguing. Rachelle, do you think this might help document who we've served for the grant proposals you're working on?"

Rachelle nodded. "Let's give it a try. 'Barry, come with me and I'll get you started.'"

Barry and I volunteered every Saturday. By then the smells that I'd noticed on my first visit no longer mattered. I reviewed Medicaid eligibility rules as he made out cards. I was so efficient at my day job that, when I wasn't traveling out of town, I'd finish work by early afternoon and volunteer at the clinic the rest of the day.

After I interviewed each client to document their medical needs, I called the Medicaid office. It took hours and lots of phone calls to get each person enrolled, but the payoff was worth it. Medicaid helped many of them qualify to get the additional medical help they needed.

Barry also made quick progress. After he had everything ready, he invited us for a demonstration. I sat at the end of the table waiting for the big reveal. *I hope this works.*

"Okay, Rachelle," Jack pointed to the cards Barry had provided. "Ask him a question."

She crossed her arms under the brown serape that covered her petite frame like a blanket. "How many women do we serve and how many children under the age of eighteen? I need this for my grant proposal."

Barry started sorting. The system worked like a dream. In a few seconds he answered her questions adding, "Fewer than a third of this group are on Medicaid, and 80 percent of them live within twenty blocks of the clinic."

Rachelle and Jack laughed. Rachelle asked, "Now remind me again how you all found us?"

"Speaking of that," I said, "My company provides doctors free sample drugs and vitamins. Jack, if you tell me what the clinic can use and sign these forms, I'll bring them the next time I come."

That night when I settled in bed, I felt better than I had in months. Maybe I could help clients in the clinic while I remained selling pharmaceuticals. Perhaps I didn't have to be Sister Maura to feel at home and do good in the world.

With that I turned off the light and went to sleep.

CHANGING TO A different job than Barry had its advantages. I realized his eyes had constantly followed me at work. He stared at me as I walked down the hall. He still turned up at my apartment most nights when I got home from work. It felt as if he wanted more time with me than I was comfortable with.

"Barry, how about we set up some specific date nights when we can be together? I need more time on my own."

He paused, his eyes growing moist. "Sure," he said. "Whatever you want."

He didn't get the message. Most nights he still turned up at my apartment door. "Just checking in," he'd say.

"Barry, we agreed to a few dates a week. You need to stop dropping by all the time."

"Okay." He walked down the hallway with slumped shoulders.

A few nights later he knocked on my door with an empty sugar bowl in his hand. "Can I borrow a cup of sugar?"

I filled the bowl and brought it back to him as he stood in the doorway.

"That's it, Barry. I need to end our relationship. I appreciate who you are and what we've shared. But you want more of me than I want to give. It's over. We're over." I closed the door.

I did miss him after that. I missed his humor and his heartfelt care for me. I didn't like how our relationship had ended, but I knew I had done the right thing. I had listened to my inner voice and trusted myself. I couldn't understand why he wasn't willing to give me more space. When I asked a friend what she thought, she said, "Maura, he's in love with you. He's thinking with his heart."

I realized I had a lot to learn about love and friendship. I wasn't ready to commit to a long-term relationship—not with Barry and not with anyone. I needed to find out more about who I was. I wanted to be open to love and adventure but not yet.

No, not yet.

fourteen

IRELAND

VOLUNTEERING AT THE free clinic helped me feel better about working for a pharmaceutical company. Before that, I'd only worked for nonprofit organizations, and being in the convent hadn't prepared me to help a large corporation make money. When I thought about what was most important to me, I knew what that was—I wanted to earn enough money to visit Ireland. Dad's family was there and so was Mom's. Mom and Aunt Jo had talked often about their cousins in Sligo. I'd listened as they chatted about Joseph Tivnan, Vincent, and the other cousins. I wanted to meet them in person. I may have left my convent family behind, but I still had Irish family I hadn't met yet.

One day in 1978, when I'd saved enough money, I visited Mom. "I want to go to Ireland to visit our relatives. I've saved up enough for our plane tickets. Will you come with me?"

"No, Maura. I won't go. All my relatives are dead."

After a few minutes of trying to coax her to go with me, I asked her for the address of her cousin Joseph. I wanted to arrange to see him. She was shocked that I knew about him.

"Mom, you and Aunt Jo talked about him all the time."

She sighed, probably wondering what else I remembered from those visits to the monastery where she and Aunt Jo shared stories across the metal screen. I copied it from her address book:

>Joseph Tivnan
>Silverhill
>Balinfull
>County Sligo
>Ireland

I WROTE HIM and, a few weeks later, he wrote back with the day and time we could meet. "Come. I'll meet you in front of Lang's on the main road in Grange. We'd love to meet you."

Before the plane landed, my eyes teared up as it circled over the patchwork quilt of lush greens. I wished my mother had joined me and that my father was still alive. I swallowed hard as the wheels hit the tarmac. I knew another adventure was about to begin.

Luckily, Aunt Maggie was in Ireland at the same time and met me at Shannon Airport. She introduced me to Dad's family starting with their brother, Eugene; his wife, Anna Mary; and their eight children. Uncle Eugene, a bear of a man, had a wide face, a ruddy complexion, and shining blue eyes. He looked nothing like my father.

After we settled down with tea, he teased me, "Maura, say your name."

"What do you mean?" I could tell he had something in mind.

"Just say your name, the whole of it." He waited, tapping the ash of his cigarette into a blackened marble ashtray as the peat burning in the fireplace gave off the earthy aroma of ancient times.

"Maura Bridget Clare Doherty." I pronounced Doherty like I always did, "Dar-ity." The first part sounded like the "dar" in "dar-ling."

"Ah, ye are surely a Yank, aren't ye? Ye don't even know how to say your own name." He stubbed out his cigarette. "It's Dar-<u>her</u>-tee." He put a quick exhaled breath into the "her."

I practiced it a few times as he laughed, his cheeks growing redder.

"All right," he said catching his breath, wiping his eyes. "I'll just call ye the Americana. Ye are not just a Yank, ye are the Americana." His wife, Anna Mary, and their children looked on, not sure what to make of this new cousin from America.

"I'll keep practicing, Uncle Eugene. But you have to plan a trip to visit us, won't you? We'd love to have you and your family come to New York."

His eyes hardened. "I promised myself I would never set foot in America for what it did to your father."

"What do you mean?" The air in the room seemed to stand still. I knew that Dad had worked hard and died much too young. Raising seven children and working so many jobs had exhausted him. But why would that be a reason for Uncle Eugene not to visit us?

"Your father was a gentle person, Maura, as gentle as a man could be. He never worked a day in his life in Ireland. Why, he'd go out in the rowboat with his book, a sandwich, and a fishing pole. He'd be out all day, come back with the sandwich ate, the book read, with not a fish to be seen, but looking quite well rested. Then he left for America. When he came back to visit, he was as nervous as a cat. He'd jump at the drop of a pin. No, Maura. I promised myself I'd never set foot in America for what it did to your father."

I took a breath and remembered how Dad would fall asleep at the kitchen table with his head in his hands, a cigarette burning between his fingers. He was always tired, but nervous? That, I hadn't known.

That night as I fell asleep, I imagined my father out in that rowboat on a peaceful lake, fish jumping here and there, some swimming lazy circles in the shadows. There'd be a slight breeze, a mist of rain with sun peeking through the clouds. He'd cast his pole overhead, the lure striking the surface of the water, sinking down. He'd prop the pole under the seat, open his book, and start to read. Hours later, he'd nibble a corner of bread and, before he turned the page, the bread was finished. He'd check the line, put on fresh bait, a wriggling worm dug from the garden. Then he'd cast again and settle in.

At one point he may have asked himself if he should he move to America. His uncle, his mother's brother, had written him a letter. "Come to New York. I will sponsor you and help you find work."

I imagined him putting the letter back into his pocket, wondering what he should do.

In 1930, my father was twenty years old. Cousin Mary had told me he wanted to go to college. In 1930 Saint Patrick's College in Maynooth, County Kildare was only open to men studying for the priesthood. According to my cousin, Dad refused to become a priest. He decided to go to America instead. He loved books and wanted to learn, but not that way. He knew he would miss his family and the lake but made plans to leave Ireland.

I imagined that, just before he rowed back to shore, the

fishing line went taut. *Dinner*, he'd think, as he reeled in a thrashing pike, wondering what awaited him in America.

◇

MY MOTHER'S COUSIN Joseph Tivnan asked to meet me outside of Lang's, a small space that combined a grocery store, pub, and post office. Aunt Maggie's husband, Uncle Jimmy, said he'd drive me there the day before to make sure he knew the way. Then we'd go back the following day to meet the family.

"Uncle Jimmy, they expect us tomorrow, not today. Can't we wait until then?"

"Ah, Maura, they'll never know we're there. We'll just see how long it takes so we're on time tomorrow."

After a few hours of driving, we got out of the car, sat on stools on the pub side, and ordered Guinness. The air smelled of beer mingled with cigarette and pipe smoke. A few minutes later a man came in and walked over to the post office window. I thought nothing of it until I felt a presence behind me. When I turned around, there he was, rocking from one foot to another as he twisted a tweed cap in his hands, his eyes trained on his shoes.

"Are ye the Yank?" he muttered in a thick brogue. His eyes darted to mine then back to the floor as if the answer lay in the wood under his feet.

"Yes. I'm the Yank."

"Oh, Kathleen isn't ready, she isn't now, is she? Ye were to come tomorrow, weren't ye? Ye are a day early."

I lowered my head to meet his gaze and said, "We *will* be here tomorrow. We just came today to make sure we knew the roads. Please tell me who you are."

He raised his head and looked at me. "I'm your cousin Vincent Tivnan and Kathleen is my wife. We look forward to seeing ye tomorrow." With this he straightened out his cap, put it on his head, nodded, and left.

I turned to my uncle. "So much for sneaking into town."

The next day we drove back, and there was Cousin Joseph waiting for us in front of Lang's. When he saw me, he started to cry.

"Joseph," I said, as I walked over to him, "why are you crying?"

"Ah, Maura. Ye look just like your mother."

We both cried and hugged and cried some more.

"Well, lass. We'd better be off to meet the rest of them or Kathleen will wonder what happened to us."

I knew about cousins Joseph, Vincent, and Kathleen but who were "the rest of them"?

When we got to a house a short distance away, Vincent came out to meet us, gave me a big smile, shook my hand, and introduced us to his wife, Kathleen, and their children; then introduced me to Cousin John Pat and his wife, Kathleen, and their children; then to Cousin Michael, his wife, Marion, and their children; then to Cousin Bernie, his wife, Sadie, and their children. By the time he finished, I was surrounded by more than a dozen cousins. My mother's dead relatives were alive and well. We shared a wonderful meal of sliced meats, tomatoes, lettuce, several kinds of bread, and for dessert, trifle, a delicious cross between custard and a fruit tart. The room filled with laughter and conversation as we ate. Then, the instruments came out—accordions, fiddles, mandolins, guitars, and a bodhran, which was an Irish drum. A young girl got up and danced a jig, her dark hair bouncing off her shoulders as she swung around the room. My feet tapped to the music.

Joseph leaned over. "Ah, Maura. Can ye do an Irish step?"

"I used to," I said, remembering the Irish dance lessons I'd taken many years before.

"Then go. That's Breedge, John Pat's daughter. Go on, now." He pointed to the young girl who was still twirling, her feet a blur of dance steps.

I got up, stood next to Breedge who threw me a smile and asked if I knew a reel. I nodded and we danced around that dining room, while the cousins clapped and played their instruments. When we finished we bowed and everyone applauded. Hours later, after all the food had been eaten, it was time to leave. I felt as if I was leaving part of my heart with them. I thought about Mom and how she must miss her cousins. How she had put on a brave face to ease the pain of having left them all behind.

Joseph drove us back to Lang's. By then tears were rolling down my cheeks. This dear man, who so missed my mother and her sister Jo. Saying goodbye to him was like leaving a part of my own family behind.

A FEW DAYS later Uncle Jimmy and Aunt Maggie drove me back to the airport.

Aunt Maggie hugged me close. "Tell you mother I'll call her when I get home in a few weeks. I love ye, dear Maura." She held me at an arm's length. "I'm glad we got to spend time together. Now, off with ye." With this she let me go. Passengers carrying shopping bags and small luggage hurried past me as I placed my bag on the conveyor. When I turned around, she and my uncle were gone.

When I landed in New York, Mom met me at the airport with my sister Colleen.

Mom's hazel eyes found mine. "How was everyone, Maura?" She took a breath. "How is Joseph? And Vincent?"

I remembered her saying her relatives had all died. She had locked her memories of them away. It must have been too difficult for her to share stories of her Irish family. The pain of leaving them must have felt too close, even after all these years.

I said, "All your dead relatives said to say hello."

"Oh, Maura."

Then, I told her everything. "We had an amazing time at your cousin Vincent's house. All the Tivnan cousins were there. And Joseph cried when he met me. He said I looked just like you." I told her who had been there, praised Breedge's step dancing and cousin Kathleen's hospitality. When I finished she lowered her head and we cried together, there in that airport, each of us with our memories of love and loss, of family newly found and left behind.

◆

MORE THAN TWO decades later, after Mom, Joseph, Vincent, and several other cousins had died, I returned to Grange. This time I was with my husband, Ken—a master welder and metal artist—whom I had married in 2001. This was the first time we were visiting Ireland together, and he was eager to meet my Irish family.

We arrived in front of Lang's with a photo of my mother's former home. My brother Michael had taken it a week earlier before he met us for a family reunion in Ireland. As we stood in Lang's doorway, loss and heartbreak pressed in on me as

I thought about Mom. I gathered myself and walked inside. The miniscule space was now all pub with stools lining three sides with a restaurant next door. Every seat was taken, and the room echoed with conversation until we stepped inside. For a moment, I was too choked up to speak. I handed the photo to my husband and he spoke.

"Hi everyone. My wife Maura's mother is from Grange. This is a photo of the house where her mother grew up. Can anyone tell us where the house is?"

I took the photo and held it up. "My name is Maura and my mother, Kathleen Tivnan, lived here. I wonder if you could help us find her house. My brother took this photo, and we'd like to see where it is."

The man who sat nearest me took the photo and passed it along. As it moved from person to person, some people nodded, and a few whispered something I couldn't hear. When it got to the last man, he handed the photo back to me.

"And what do you want with the house if you find it?"

"I just want to take my own picture of it from the outside for a keepsake."

He looked around the bar and everyone nodded in agreement. "Well, that's Wee Willie's house. It's just down the main road across from the chemist."

I thanked them and turned to leave.

Then a women called out, "Aren't you going to see Breedge?"

"Breedge is still here? I'll get her phone number and call her."

The woman laughed. "Ah, no need to call. Why, she's always home. Just knock on her door," and she gave me directions to the house.

First, I went to my mother's house. I stood on the edge of the main road gazing at the home where my mother had grown up. I took in its white stucco walls, brown tiled roof, and blue and red trimmed windows. She had lived here with three sisters and a brother as her father worked as a shoemaker and her mother kept house. She had no idea her sister Jo would become a nun; another sister, Mai, would die from tuberculosis; and another sister, Rita, would join her in America along with their brother Jim. Her parents would die a year after Mom married my father. I swallowed hard and walked across the road to Cousin Breedge's house.

I KNOCKED ON Breedge's door. When she opened the door, I told her who I was.

"Are you the one who danced with me many years ago?"

"Yes, Breedge. That was me."

"I always wondered if you'd come back. Come in, come in."

"Breedge," I said after the tea was poured, "How did you know it was me at your door?"

"Didn't your brother Michael come to call just last week? I asked him which of his sisters might have done Irish step dancing, but he didn't seem to know."

I laughed and explained that my brother Michael was hard of hearing. When the folks at Lang's brought him to Breedge's for tea, he'd had no idea they were related.

Breedge and I shared laughter and tears as we spoke about family, those who were still with us and those who had passed, and the room pulsated with memories of two girls, one very young and one older, dancing together so many years ago.

fifteen

HIGHLANDER CENTER

IN 1979, A few months after I'd returned from my first trip to Ireland, Barry sent me information on a job at Nashville's Center for Health Services. The first three months would include work with the Highlander Research Center in East Tennessee. This was my chance. Maybe, just maybe, I would know what to say.

I applied for the job and Barry wrote a recommendation. (I was grateful that even though he and I were no longer dating, we were still friends.) They flew me to Nashville for an interview. The center was housed in a century-old home, and, as I made my way onto the front porch, I noticed two people sitting on a swing, engrossed in conversation. Flowering magnolia trees surrounded me with fragrance. I flashed back to my stolen time reading *Gone with the Wind,* to Scarlett O'Hara and the magnolia blossoms she loved so much. I wondered how it all fit together—Nashville and the South and this nonprofit dedicated to supporting medically underserved communities.

I pulled open the screen door and a woman with red hair

and oversized glasses showed me into the Director's office. The director Jonathan's shirtsleeves were rolled up as he scanned the paperwork in front of him. He gave me a half smile and reached out to shake my hand.

When our hands touched, I heard a big fat "*NO*" inside my head. I stared at him. He gestured for me to sit down.

Had the NO been a warning? About him? About the job? I sank into a chair and made myself breathe. *Later. I'll think about it later.*

He asked questions about who I was and why I'd applied for the job.

"I have an undergraduate degree in biology. I taught high school science and worked on demonstrations against closing the local hospital."

The whole time, I thought, why the *NO*? It had surprised me. Was my inner spirit warning me? If so, warning me about what? The Center for Health Services had a good reputation, and Jonathan was a respected scholar and activist. If I wanted to work with Highlander, this was the way to do it. They were both nonprofit organizations, and Highlander had something I craved—a group of committed activists who fought for civil rights. I wanted to join their fight against environmental pollution, even if it meant committing to a longer-term job with another allied organization.

I wanted the job, even though the big, fat *NO* lingered in the air.

◆

THE NEXT DAY Jonathan and I drove five hours to East Tennessee to the final interview with the Highlander Center. The view along the highway was punctuated by roadway signs advertising honey baked ham and cigarettes. He pointed to the Cumberland Mountains in the distance. "We work with a community clinic and several groups fighting strip mining out there." He turned the car on to the familiar gravel road, past the garden, round buildings and a handful of other houses tucked behind trees that swayed in the breeze. The air smelled like fresh mown grass.

We walked in, met the staff, and sat in rocking chairs in the same circular room where Barry and I had sat a year earlier. When Helen Lewis, a social anthropologist and educator, shook my hand, I felt welcome, wanted. Her soft brown hair fell in waves around her head and her eyes sparked with curiosity. She had a grant funded by the National Science Foundation for three educational forums in Appalachia. If she hired me, I'd coordinate the event in Kingsport in Upper East Tennessee. The center would provide three months of salary to organize the forum before the job transitioned to support community health centers.

Helen's smile radiated warmth. "Maura. Tell me more about why you want to do this work." Her Virginia drawl was soft, her eyes intense, but there was something else there, too—a commitment to do what was right.

As she spoke, I felt myself open. I knew I was on the cusp of something big. This time I told her about my students in the Bronx. How their families had no health insurance, how parents worked two and three jobs. How my students started rent strikes to force landlords to fix holes in floors and leaking water pipes. How they showed me how to fight for what was right. I didn't mention the convent or God or how I was searching for meaning in my new Catholic-free life. As I spoke I was filled with joy. I knew I was in the right place.

She smiled. "I wrote this grant so folks might tell their stories about pollution and health. People need to tell their stories. Together they'll find ways to improve their lives."

Tell stories. Yes, I want this job. She went on to describe that the grant would hire two other women to organize public forums in Charleston, West Virginia and Harlan, Kentucky. The goal for each was the same as Kingsport: to provide citizens the opportunity to discuss how air and water quality affected their health.

They hired me a few weeks later. I trusted I would find the Yes in this opportunity. I promised myself I would keep an eye on Jonathan, just in case the *NO* had been warning me about him.

⟡

AFTER I PACKED the car with my few belongings, I drove ten hours from DC to Nashville. Several times I stopped and peeled myself out of the driver's seat. My heart pounded as I thought about what waited for me in Nashville.

Will I know what to do?

Then I got back into the car.

When I arrived, I discovered that the staff had gone for the day, but the office door was unlocked. Because I had limited funds, I slept on a couch in the back room until the next morning when I heard doors opening and footsteps down the hall. I got up, found the bathroom, braced myself, and walked into the main office.

"Hi, I'm Maura, the new coordinator for the Highlander project."

The first one who reached out his hand said, "I'm John

with the farm project. This is Lindsey." A willowy blonde waved at me from the coffee machine on the counter, flashing a brilliant smile. "Welcome. We heard you were joining us. Glad to meet you."

Jamie Cohen was next. "Finally. Jonathan told me about you." She gave me a hug, the top of her head just reaching my chin. When she stepped back she grinned and said, "Get ready for some good work and lots of fun." When I told her I'd slept in the office, she groaned. "No way. You're welcome to stay with me whenever you're in Nashville. I know how it is working on these out-of-town projects."

A few days later I drove to Highlander to talk about the project. Helen, Juliet (the lead researcher whom I'd also met on my first visit), Maxine Kenny, a photographer activist, and I sat down on yet more rocking chairs, which I came to learn were part of Highlander's rich history of bringing folks together.

Maxine's hair was pulled into a thick braid that hung over her shoulder.

Helen's smile widened when she looked at us, as if she relished the adventure that was about to unfold. "Well, Maura. You're the newest one here and you haven't yet been to Kingsport." She paused. "The air in Kingsport smells." With that she wrinkled her nose and shook her head. "All of it from chemicals. My friends there are sick. We think it's from breathing the air."

Everyone nodded. Juliet looked down and wrote something in her notebook. Helen and Maxine held my gaze.

Then Helen continued. "Maura, keep your eyes and ears open. Most folks just want to live in a healthy environment, and you're there to help them with that." She had a strong belief that the town's distinctive odor came from polluting companies that made money by discarding waste into the air and water. I would be there to question those practices. She ended by saying, "My friend Connie offered you room and board in Kingsport while you plan the conference. Here's her name and contact information along with names of the folks who have agreed to help."

As I took the paper from her hands, I realized I was nervous. After all, I was from the Bronx. I had taught biology and health education to Catholic school girls. I had updated doctors on medications. I'd never worked on pollution problems. But with Helen and Highlander's support, I believed I could do the job.

✧

HELEN, JULIET, MAXINE and I talked the rest of the morning about the goal of the project, the town, and about Helen's contacts before I got in my car and drove north. I tried to conjure up visuals of what Helen had said and to imagine the smells that she'd described. But it was difficult. I wondered how bad it might be. When I arrived in Kingsport, I knew right away that it was bad. Very bad. The stench that wafted through the window was downright nauseating. I pulled over, rolled up the windows, and headed toward town. As I got closer the smell thickened, like someone had composted dead fish and decaying meat and encased the town in it. The Tennessee Eastman plant, Eastman Kodak's chemical plant, a leader in the world of plastics, was on one side of the road. Less than a mile away sat the Holston Army Ammunition plant, which I'd been told, was chock full of ordnance waiting for the next war. The town also had a paper mill, a concrete plant, and dozens of other industries. I was in the upper right corner of Tennessee surrounded by poisoned air.

Why Helen had hired me to organize a two-day conference on health and pollution still mystified me. From the nasty smell, I could tell why the town might need a discussion on the subject, but I'd never organized a conference. I'd learned how to pretend to meditate in the early hours in bucolic chapels, and I'd excelled in convincing rambunctious teenage girls to turn in homework. But figuring out how to craft a public forum around pollution? Helen had promised that Highlander would take care of the research on industrial pollution. I was tasked with forming a local committee to plan the two-day conference.

I got started by calling everyone on the list Helen had given me. I might have left Jesus and my community of Sisters behind, but I hadn't left my work ethic. I was an energetic, motivated young woman from the Bronx with a can-do attitude. I was also driving a Japanese car in a small town replete with American flags.

I placed one phone call after another, introducing myself, and asking each person if they wanted to be on the planning committee.

"Hi. Mrs. Collins? I'm working with Helen Lewis at the Highlander Center on the environmental forum in Kingsport. Do you have a few minutes to talk?"

She said, "Why, yes. My husband and I are both very interested. Helen had told us to expect your call. Just tell us where and we can meet."

The others I called agreed as well. They all wanted to plan a public discussion of how pollution affected the health of Kingsport residents.

Without the smell, Kingsport might have been idyllic. It was situated amidst lush hillsides and flowing rivers. The neighboring town of Johnson City hosted East Tennessee State University and its medical center, potential collaborators for our conference. Unfortunately, timing wasn't in our favor. It was 1979, decades before environmental awareness and strong environmental protection legislation. All I had on my side was the Highlander Center and the folks who were interested in working on the conference.

I called Jonathan to tell him I'd started the work in Kingsport.

"Glad you made it," he said. "Remember you have only three months to hold the conference. Then you can start working with the community clinics."

I agreed, hung up the phone, and put him out of my mind. Work with clinics needed to wait until the Kingsport project was completed. And the *NO* that had shouted at me when I shook his hand still rang in my ears.

✧

I INVITED THE members of the new planning committee to Connie's for our first meeting. By the time we met, I'd almost gotten used to the fetid air that seeped through the closed doors and windows. The day of the meeting, sunlight shone on the pitcher of iced tea that waited for us in the middle of the oak table.

"Hello, everyone. Welcome to the first meeting of the Kingsport planning committee. I'm Maura Doherty. I've been hired by Helen Lewis at the Highlander Center to help you plan a two-day conference on health and pollution. Each of you has expressed interest in helping us out. Why don't we go around the table so you can tell us who you are and why you've joined us?"

Tom Collins, a mild-mannered man with a slight build and thinning brown hair, turned to his wife, Mildred, then back to the group. "Many of you know me from church or the community center." Everyone nodded. He sat up straighter. "I love Kingsport. Was born and raised here." With that he put his hands flat on the table. "But I'm tired of being sick all the time, of my kids being sick, every year, pneumonia, bronchitis, you name it. Mildred and I were glad to meet Helen, and we want to do what we can to help our town." His shoulders relaxed and his hands went to his lap as if his most important task was taken care of.

The room filled with uh-huhs and nodding heads. His wife, Mildred, reached over to pat her husband's hand, "This is for the children," she said. "Tom and I have had a good life, but what will happen to our children, and God willing, our grandchildren who grow up with this nasty air? It's not right. That's why I'm here."

Mary, an elementary school teacher whose bulk spilled out from the sides of her chair, spoke next. "Those are my students you're talking about. They're out sick a lot and, when they are in school, it's hard for them to concentrate with the chemical smell that fills the classroom. Even closing windows doesn't help. I want to do what I can to get the town and the companies that pollute to take responsibility for it."

Next came Billie. She looked at each of us with a smile. "Like many of you, I was born and raised here. My family and grandchildren all live here. I'm here for them. Like you, I'm darn tired of being sick and watching my kin get sick. It's time to speak up and talk about our quality of life. And how the air in Kingsport takes away from that." As she finished, the grandfather clock in the corner tolled the hour.

I looked at them. "I take those chimes as a sign of good luck. Now, let's get started." I had my allies. Now to tackle the rest of the town and to find others who might support us.

The job called for networking. The committee members agreed to talk to family, friends, pastors, fellow churchgoers, and others. I said I would meet with the Chamber of Commerce, healthcare professionals, and representatives of industry, the university, and the media. The Chamber of Commerce, however, turned into a dead end. When I met with the head of the local chapter, he shook his head and interrupted me before I'd finished my summary.

"No, Miss Doherty." He clenched his lips before he continued, his crew cut so stiff it looked like he had starched it. "It's not in our best interest to support your . . . cause. We support local business, not outsiders who claim to know better than us. Thank you. Goodbye." With that, he got up and left the room.

I thought Bronx teenagers were tough. As I pushed my chair back, I looked out the window at the towering trees, barren branches that would spring to life in a few months. *Just give it time, Maura.* Unfortunately, every group I subsequently met with also declined to advertise or support our event. After several rejections, I called Helen.

She said, "Kingsport has a long history, and we're just a small part of it. Stick close to your local people. Your job is to listen and give them a chance to tell their stories."

That night I called Tom. "Why do you think there's so much resistance to this conference?"

"Well, Maura, to put it straight out, we're a company town. You know, where one company tells everyone else what to do. In other parts of Tennessee, it's the coal mine. Here it's Eastman. They hire over 15,000 people to make chemicals and plastic. And we're a town of 30,000! People come from all over the region to work there. They pay well so employees don't ask questions, and all the other companies in town do what Eastman says. And what we're a-doing is asking questions. Everyone else sticks together. They smell the nasty air and go back to work. Most Friday nights, Eastman's community center runs family night with free movies, popcorn, and games. That keeps everyone coming back."

All I could say was, "Wow." What Helen had told me about Eastman hadn't hit home until now.

"And that's not all. Did you know that it snows here in summer?"

"What do you mean?"

"White dust falls from the sky and lands on our houses and cars and everything else. Only it doesn't melt. It's pollution that gets mixed up in the air and comes down and corrodes everything it touches. Takes the paint right off. So, we repaint our cars and homes lots of times to make the damage go away. Just imagine what it's a-doing to our lungs when we breathe it in. This is serious stuff. In Kingsport the smells and the dust and all of it means that someone's making money and we're paying for it with our health."

I'd never come across anything like the extent of this pollution, and the courage Tom and the others on the committee had in challenging the status quo.

I called Billie next and asked how she was doing. After she told me about some of the folks she'd talked to and why they were worried about helping her, she said. "Think about this, Miss Maura. Years ago, Eastman had an explosion. My grandfather lost an arm, others were killed, and lots were injured. The company paid everyone off and life went on. And it's not just the air we're worried about. When we were growing up, we lived by the river. They dumped everything into the water, but we didn't know it. My sister went for a swim one day and came out screaming her head off. Her skin was blistered, like she'd bathed in acid. We got her to the hospital, and I'll never forget the pain in her eyes as all her skin peeled off. No one could tell us what had happened. She was never the same after that."

Chills ran down my arms. "Billie, I'm so sorry."

"Miss Maura, this town needs to know that we mean business. I'm glad you're here to help us do that."

Free movies and popcorn wouldn't save Kingsport or the families at the Eastman community center. But maybe an open discussion on the impact of pollution on health would help raise the questions that would lead to solutions. Maybe.

I knew I was an outsider driving a car from a country that many had fought in World War II. Not only that, I also had a Bronx accent and worked for the Highlander Center that fought for civil rights. Kingsport hired people of color but relegated them to the lowest paying jobs. Every time I hit a roadblock, I called Helen. Her calm demeanor and confidence assured me that we were on the right track. But even she hadn't prepared me for what happened next.

At the next meeting Billie asked, "Has anyone noticed a problem with their phone? Maybe a crackling or buzzing on the line?"

We looked at each other. For the past week the phone calls I'd made from Connie's had lots of static; the phone company couldn't say why. Now the others chimed in about the same problem.

After a long silence Tom asked, "Do you think it's possible they're tapping our phones?"

After a moment, everyone nodded.

Tom asked. "I'm a-wondering about something else. Has anyone noticed a dark sedan following you when you drive around town? I sure have. Several times."

Mary spoke up. "I thought I was imagining things, but, yes, I've seen a dark-colored car, maybe a dark blue? It follows me when I drive to school and when I drive home. Anyone else?"

Billie said, "Well, I mostly drive to church or to the store, so they probably don't think I'm worth following."

We laughed. But it was the first time I felt fear in that room. My heart raced as I thought about the tactics that the "other side" might be using against us. Mary tapped her pen on her pad. Tom reached for Mildred's hand as we sat there, reviewing the evidence. Was someone really following us and listening to our phone conversations?

Then, in an instant, doubt turned to determination.

Billie spoke first. "I think it's time to take a vote. Are all of us willing to continue?" She paused. "I'm here for good. Anyone else?"

Everyone said yes.

◆

A MONTH BEFORE the conference, the local radio station agreed to interview me. I'd memorized the key points I wanted to emphasize and, at first, it went well.

When the On Air sign turned green, the radio host welcomed me to the program. "Miss Doherty, thanks for being with us today. Why don't you tell us about the conference you're organizing?"

"Yes. We're sponsored by a grant from the National Science Foundation through the Highlander Center. Our goal is to discuss how pollution might be affecting the health of people in Kingsport. It's a free two-day public forum for anyone who wants to attend." I went on to give specifics on the time and place.

He paused. "Miss Doherty, isn't it true that you are a Communist, here to shut down our industry and take away our jobs?"

I wasn't prepared for that. Naïve me hadn't anticipated the radio host firing all barrels at me.

"No, sir. This is a public forum sponsored by the Science for the People program of the National Science Foundation. Our goal is to discuss the scientific evidence linking health concerns with pollution."

The rest of the interview was a blur. He lied and used fear and intimidation to turn his listeners against me and the project. I was so steamed when I left the station that I did what I needed to do to calm down.

I called Helen.

She said, "The more they say those things, the more scared they are. Now you're a troublemaker like the rest of us."

For the first time in days I smiled, and the headache

that had surged during the interview receded. I was in good company.

Then she continued. "Now you know that you're getting somewhere. Why don't I come down and pick you up and bring you back to Highlander with me? We have a training going on and there'll be music tonight."

I quickly agreed.

When Helen arrived, she sat across from me at Connie's kitchen table, her calm expression belying the fire in her eyes as she talked about the issues plaguing Appalachia. "You know, the work we're doing in Kingsport isn't so different than our work with coal miners. When we brought miners from Kentucky to Wales and sat them down with Welsh miners, they were amazed at how much they had in common. People at the top underestimate the power of people who struggle for safe jobs and communities. Those workers were from different countries, but when it came to work and family, they spoke the same language. Kingsport's not so different. It's controlled by the chemical industry that's used to getting its way."

That night, Guy and Candie Carawan led everyone in songs celebrating human and civil rights. As we sang "We Shall Overcome," I thought of Tom and Mildred, Mary and Billie, and all those courageous enough to fight for a better life. I believed "deep in my heart" that we would overcome the forces against us.

One of the forces against me included Jonathan in Nashville. When I drove back to Nashville to update him on our progress, the big, fat *NO* reared its head again. He glared at me. "Maura, your three months are up. Why aren't you finished with the conference? This is not acceptable."

Even when I told him about the obstacles we were facing, he wasn't satisfied. "I'm going to cut off your salary. You're just dragging your feet. This conference is going to be a failure."

I knew what to do. I called Helen and asked her to talk with him.

She reassured him that, despite the delay, we were on track to host the two-day conference with keynote speakers and panel discussions on how pollution damages health. Helen's source at the local newspaper told her that the editor wasn't sure if he'd support the conference. He'd drafted two editorials—one supported us, but the other didn't. We had to wait and see which one he'd print.

A week later, Tom and Mildred arrived late to the last planning meeting. Tom avoided looking at us as he stood in the doorway. Mildred's eyes were trained on her hands, her fingers pointing like arrows against her sides. Tom looked up, his gaze on me. "I need to resign from the committee. Mildred and I both." His fists were clenched in front of him, knuckles blazing white. His eyes filled with tears as he stood there, then turned and left the room with Mildred at his side. I followed them to the front door.

"Tom, do you want to tell me what happened?"

He took a breath and nodded. "They threatened me. That's what. My boss told me I'd lose my job if I kept working on the conference." Mildred reached over and took his hand as he continued. "Not just that. Mildred would lose her job too, and so would my son and daughter-in-law. I just can't hurt them like that. I just can't."

I paused. "Tom, you're right. Everything we do is about protecting family. You have to put them first. Thanks for all you and Mildred did. Is it all right if I tell the others?"

He whispered, "Yes," as if it cost him everything.

Mildred moved her hand to the small of his back and we stood there for a moment, knowing that evil was at work. Prayer is not just reserved for the holy. In that moment, Tom and Mildred were the human prayers offered up against evil.

When he raised his head, his eyes flashed with anger. And when he reached out to shake my hand it was hot to the touch, like he was on fire.

I went back and told the others what had happened. "Be careful. They're going to do whatever it takes to stop you." All we could do was wait and see what would happen.

That's when history intervened. Two weeks before the conference, the Three Mile Island nuclear power plant in Pennsylvania had a meltdown. The entire country, no less the world, suddenly realized that what industry had been saying about safety was a lie. Even though Kingsport lacked nuclear power, it had more than its share of chemical plants that gave the same empty promises about safety. The day the conference began I ran out to get the newspaper. My hands were shaking as I opened to the editorial page. I was shocked. The editor didn't just support the conference, he also likened its organizers it to the patriots of the American Revolution. "... questioning old ways of doing business that might threaten the very health of our town."

I called Helen and laughed. "To think that a nuclear meltdown helped us."

Later that night as I sat on Connie's porch swing, bundled in a blanket against the chilly night, I thought about the cost of courage. How much it cost people like Tom and Mildred, Billie and Mary to fight for what was right. Shame on the bullies who threatened these heroes who wanted to make their community safer. Even if Jonathan didn't support me, the folks on the Kingsport committee did. They were a big, fat YES!

◆

IT WAS TIME. The committee members had the registration table ready. I was relieved when a dozen people filed into the conference room, then a few dozen more, then more, until there was a line out the door and all the seats were filled.

I turned to Helen. "I can't believe what's happening."

"Believe it, Maura. Trust the people to do what's right."

The speakers were excellent. The panel discussions were informative and full of ideas on how the town might move to more environmentally friendly forms of waste disposal. But my proudest moment came at the beginning. Just before Mary stepped up to the microphone to welcome everyone, a couple came down the aisle, beaming smiles left and right. Tom and Mildred had returned.

Tom walked up to Mary and gestured to the microphone. "May I?"

I don't remember everything he said. It might have been the overhead lighting, but I'm sure that an orb of white light surrounded him as he spoke. ". . . nothing will stop me and my fellow citizens from asking questions. I'm proud to be a member of this committee. Now, enjoy the conference." He handed the microphone back to Mary, nodded at Billie and me, and took a seat in the front row alongside Mildred, who beamed a million-watt smile.

The conference linked citizens who questioned how industrial waste was handled, and it laid the groundwork for people across the state to work together on environmental problems. It also called for a statewide effort to work for better management of industrial waste. I was thrilled at how everything had gone as the conference ended with a standing ovation.

sixteen

BUMPASS COVE

IT WAS PITCH black, three in the morning. I sat in a lawn chair, the aluminum kind that squeaked when I moved. Thousands of stars glinted overhead as the creek tumbled over rocks to my left. Why was I sitting in a lawn chair on Bumpass Cove Road in the middle of the night?

Several months after the Kingsport conference, I heard a radio report about an evacuation in Bumpass Cove, a small hamlet east of Kingsport, following floods and an explosion on a nearby landfill. I panicked. People I had worked with on the Kingsport conference lived there. Among them, two men named Hobert and Russell had become my friends as we investigated the chemicals seeping from their local landfill. I grabbed my jacket and keys, jumped into my car, and started the six-hour drive from Nashville to Upper East Tennessee. I drove fast, mile after mile, hoping state troopers wouldn't pull me over.

Please angels, let everyone be all right. I guessed what might have happened—chemicals buried on the landfill had exploded. In the beginning of the Kingsport project, I knew only a little about chemical incompatibility and how certain chemicals exploded when they were mixed together. Thanks to Highlander and the folks in Bumpass Cove, I'd received a crash course in toxic and explosive chemicals.

Time dragged as I drove, my breath coming fast as I scanned the radio for more updates, waiting for news that never came.

Finally, I was there. My heart raced as my headlights caught the edge of the dirt road that wound past Hobert's house. No lights were on. I figured he might be somewhere else after the explosion on the landfill that he and his neighbors had been fighting to clean up for years. As I pulled down the road, a flashlight beamed through my windshield. Someone in a yellow slicker waved me over.

I rolled down my window. "I'm here to see Hobert Story. I'm Maura. He knows me."

A hood covered the stranger's head and darkness enveloped the rest of him as he trained the light on me. I closed my eyes against the glare, wondering if he'd tell me to leave. "Park here. Hobert's down the road a piece."

I parked and the man disappeared into the night. Everything was quiet. All I heard was the thud-thudding in my chest and the gurgle of the creek. I got out of the car, my boots quickly finding puddles that turned to mud. *Where was Hobert?* I heard a murmur of voices before I picked out shadows that slowly became people.

I called out, "Hobert? Is Hobert Story here?"

"Who wants to know?" The familiar voice belonged to Skip Foss, Hobert's brother-in-law. He emerged from the dark, his long lean figure blending into the night.

"Maura Doherty."

I felt his stare pierce the darkness between us, along with his unspoken words. *This is our community, our business. You don't belong here.* Skip had always put on a friendly face when I visited Hobert to plan the conference, but I'd felt something else under the surface. And it hadn't been good.

"Maury, is that you? Y'all came here to help us?" And there was Hobert who called me Maury because he said it was easier to pronounce. Skip beamed a flashlight on me so Hobert could make his way over.

I choked back tears. "I heard about the explosion and evacuation on the radio. Is everyone all right?"

"Yeah, we're okay. Come sit down. It's a long drive from Nashville. Gladys, can you get Miss Maury a cup of coffee?" He led me a few feet away and sat me down in a lawn chair, a cup appearing out of nowhere, its aroma pungent.

I turned to Hobert, who sat in the chair next to me. His face blended with the night that smelled of recent rain. "Please, tell me what happened," I said.

"Well, 'member how the folks at the Highlander Center listed some of them chemicals Waste Resources was a-haulin' into the landfill? Turns out they were right. Some of them chemicals must have mixed together in a bad way when the flood came down the holler. Drums were just sitting there, rusty, leakin'. And some weren't buried deep so when the rains came and the creek flooded, that's when it happened. They exploded. Sounded like a bomb went off. Lucky it was after nightfall or some of them fellers working up there woulda' been injured. Or dead."

"What did you do then, Hobert?" My hands squeezed the coffee cup so tightly they felt like they were burning.

"Went up the road to Gene and Irma's house. They're the only ones who have a telephone. Told them to call my friend Bobby and tell him what happened. Bobby's our civil defense coordinator in Johnson City. He's the one ordered the evacuation. I went door to door and said, 'Do you believe me now? Have you had enough yet?' Even the folks who told me to keep my nose out of that landfill business said, 'We're scared, Hobe. Tell us what to do.' I said, 'Meet us here on the road. More of them trucks will be comin' down the road come daybreak. We have to stop 'em.' And that's why, Miss Maury, we're throwing ourselves a party, right here on Bumpass Cove Road."

I realized that the shadows I'd spotted were actually a few dozen folks sitting next to us in lawn chairs that were strung across the middle of the road. The smell of cedar was strong as I turned to the man on my right.

"John Wilson, is that you?" I asked. John always carried cedar that he whittled into dogs or boys or ducks, whatever mood struck him. The fragrance of cedar surrounded him wherever he went.

"Sure is, Miss Maury. Roxy's here too. Glad you could make it." I saw the faint nod of his head as he leaned toward his wife.

I felt my heart slow and my breath ease when I realized everyone was okay. No one had been hurt. I took a sip of coffee as Hobert got up to talk with someone down the line. My eyes started to close as fatigue set in. No coffee was strong enough to counteract the drop in adrenaline after fear had driven me across the state to protect my friends.

◇

THE FIRST TIME I'd talked to Hobert, we'd been sitting on his porch in rocking chairs, right after I took the job to plan the Kingsport conference. When I had asked the state environmental agency if they'd had any complaints about chemical contamination, they showed me a file full of letters from a man named Hobert Story who'd written about chemicals being dumped in a place called Bumpass Cove. I wrote to Hobert and asked if we could meet.

When I drove toward his house, maple trees blazed red along the roadside. Hobert was sitting on his front porch; the paint on his house had faded to a dull gray. He stood up, his coveralled, six-foot frame towered over me as he shook my hand and pointed to the chair next to his. Clean mountain air enveloped me as I sat down.

"Kinda y'all to come all this way."

I had the feeling that this man would make a formidable enemy or, if I was lucky, the best of allies. Bumpass Cove was in the part of Tennessee called Appalachia, known for its distrust of strangers.

His wife, Gladys, opened the screen door and emerged holding two glasses of iced tea.

Hobert nodded to her. "Gladys, this here is Maury from that there Highlander Center. She's the one invited us to that conference I told y'all about."

I hesitated to correct his pronunciation of my name, figuring we'd talk about it some other time.

"Pleased to meetcha'. Iced tea?" Gladys handed a glass to Hobert and the other one to me. I took a sip as we settled into our chairs. It was the best iced tea I'd ever tasted.

Hobert looked at the road that ran past his house. "I retired from workin' uranium mines. Moved back here to be with family and sit on this porch, listen to the creek. But then the trucks started a-comin' down the road." He pointed with his glass to the road not twenty feet from us. "Whatever they were a haulin' was nasty. I couldn't breathe. Went in the house, closed all the winders and doors, a-huffin' and puffin'. There's an old mine at the end of the holler. Someone opened a sanitary landfill up there a few years back. Meant for household trash, not chemicals. But that's what they're a burying. The state tells me it's legal." He looked at the gravel road as if he could conjure up the trucks that drove past his house. "How I read the Tennessee Code Annotated," with that he put his glass down on the table, "is that we have a right to clean air and clean water. Them bringing nasty chemicals here is just plain wrong." His eyes flashed lightning bolts.

"It sure doesn't sound right, Hobert. Why don't I have the folks at Highlander do some research on the landfill? They're good at that." I told him more about the conference and invited him to come and talk about Bumpass Cove.

"Let me see 'bout that. You say you live in Kingsport?"

"Yes, I'm staying with a friend while I organize the conference. Let me give you my address and phone number."

He laughed at that one. "Got no phone here. We're simple people and keep to ourselves. That is, until the trucks came."

As time went on, I visited him several times on that porch, sipped iced tea, and listened to the creek as he filled me in on the latest news.

One time he said, "We had ourselves a big fish kill right there in the creek." He pointed a thumb out back. "Hundreds of 'em, belly up. Water ran purple and red that day. Don't know what they dumped up on the landfill, but it ran right into the creek and killed them fish. I'm sure of it."

Every time we sat on that porch talking about what was happening, my head pounded with anger. I knew Hobert was right. Someone was making money by dumping chemicals in the holler. The staff at Highlander continued to dig deeper into what was being trucked to the landfill as I organized the conference in Kingsport. Unfortunately, 1979 lacked requirements for full disclosure to the public of waste shipments. Highlander's requests under the Freedom of Information Act would take time.

◇

AS WE CONTINUED to plan the conference, Helen asked Jonathan to add Bumpass Cove to his federal VISTA grant proposal. VISTA, Volunteers in Service to America, provided a stipend for volunteers who worked at clinic sites as well as places like Bumpass Cove. Russell Rogers and his wife, Mary Lee, signed up to share a $300 monthly stipend to educate their community on how to protect themselves against chemical contamination.

During one of my last visits to Bumpass Cove before the conference, Russell set a plate of sandwiches on the TV tray as we sat in rickety chairs under the shade of a poplar tree. The sun dappled the leaves in shadows across us like a leafy Rorschach test. I planted my feet firmly on the ground as my chair wobbled left and right. Mary Lee sat on the steps of their mobile trailer and took a sip of coffee.

"Maury, folks here are simple. We don't have much except this beautiful country around us." She smiled and nodded as she pointed to the trees around their home. "We just want what's fair and Hobert's right. We deserve better. This VISTA grant you got for us will help out. It's not good that they come in here and dump their poisons. Now," she held out the plate, "have a bologna sandwich."

HOBERT'S BROTHER-IN-LAW, Skip, and Russell were special presenters at the Kingsport conference. They showed photos of chemical drums leaking into the ground and water, as well as a Super-8 video of fish lying belly up in the creek surrounded by pools of purple, red, and orange runoff. They talked about a cousin who died after he drank from the creek, and described how the state and county wouldn't investigate any of their complaints.

Russell looked out at the audience and asked, "Can you help us?"

Panel discussions with researchers from the Oak Ridge National Laboratory detailed how chemical contamination could injure people, fish, and wildlife. Air quality experts laid out maps with suspected areas of concern around Kingsport. Dozens who attended the conference asked questions about how pollution might impact their health.

The next day, as the conference came to a close, Russell and Skip were surrounded by folks who wanted to know more about Bumpass Cove.

Russell's question haunted me as I drove back to Nashville to start my work with the clinics. Jonathan had given me a list of sites to visit and off I went, pointing my car south and west. As I drove across the state, I asked myself, *Could I help them? If there was one Bumpass Cove, could there be more?*

I decided to find out.

⋄

BACK ON THE picket line of straggly lawn chairs, dawn broke through the gray mist as folks roused from their watch. Several women cooked breakfast on makeshift stoves. I hadn't realized how hungry I was until the aroma of eggs and hash browns wafted across the road. We finished washing dishes in galvanized tubs when the first truck rumbled toward us down the road.

Hobert turned to us. "Y'all know what to do."

We sat down. John Wilson took out his penknife and started to whittle. Hobert walked up to the truck that had stopped ten feet from our chairs and nodded to the driver.

"Good mornin'. Welcome to Bumpass Cove. We're throwing ourselves a community picnic. Would you care for a cup of coffee?"

The driver looked at Hobert, then at us, then back to Hobert. "I guess."

Hobert turned and called, "Gladys, would y'all please bring this gentleman a cup a coffee?"

Gladys returned with a steaming mug. "Cream, sugar?"

The driver shook his head. "Black is fine."

I leaned over for a closer look at John's carving. This one was a dog, a hunter, nose pointed straight at the truck.

A man in blue coveralls walked alongside the truck with something in his hand. Who was he and what was he holding?

Just then a second truck pulled up and Hobert greeted the driver the way he had the first one. Gladys brought over another cup of coffee. Both drivers stepped out to talk to Hobert and, from what I overheard, they figured out they'd once gone fishing with Hobert's cousin. By then the man in coveralls had disappeared around the back of the second truck. My heart raced a little faster as I wondered if Hobert had been right when he promised there'd be no violence. Could the man in coveralls be holding a gun? After all, this was Appalachia, where gunfights were common.

Hobert had said, "I sent the men up in the hills to keep a look out. They have guns that aren't worth anythin' this far away. But it's best they're not here to rile things up."

Suddenly, the man was standing next to Hobert and greeting the drivers. "Mornin'," he said as he reached over to shake their hands. "Let me introduce myself. I'm Bobby Wright, the Civil Defense coordinator, and a county highway inspector." He leaned down and picked something up off the ground. "This here is a portable scale. And it has informed me that both your trucks are over the weight limits for the bridge you need to cross to get up to the landfill. Sorry to say, gentlemen." With that he put down the scale and pulled a pad out from his pocket. "This here is a warning. If I hear tell you or any other driver comes back down this road with loads exceeding the limit, you will be cited and could lose your commercial driver's license. Are we clear?"

The two men nodded, grumbled about what had just happened, and handed their coffee cups to Hobert who told them, "You can back up and turn around at the abandoned store just a hundred or so feet behind you. Good day, gentlemen."

After the trucks left, we all stood up and hugged and hooted over our victory. That's when it dawned on me that I was six hours from home.

Russell took me aside and asked if I felt okay to drive back. I assured him that I was, and the miles flew by with adrenaline still pumping in my system.

Hobert had confided in me that Waste Resources, the company that managed the landfill, seemed to know what

Bumpass Cove's plans were as soon as Hobert knew. It happened so often that Hobert suspected that there might be a spy in Bumpass Cove, someone close to him. Since the explosion had caught everyone by surprise, Hobert was the only one who knew about the call to the county road inspector. Time would tell if he was right in thinking that someone was telling Waste Resources about Bumpass Cove's next move.

I don't remember how it all came to a head. Maybe it was the guilt building up in the man who had betrayed his community. But a few weeks after they stopped the trucks, I got a letter from Russell with the news that Skip Foss was the snitch. Waste Resources had paid him to keep them updated on Bumpass Cove. Skip was Hobert's brother-in-law. How could he? My blood boiled as I thought about how my intuition had been right: Skip's smile had hidden something not-so-nice under the surface. As time went on, however, I thought about how folks there had only the bare essentials with which to get by. Most of them lived off the land, hunting and fishing. But, after the chemicals tainted everything, no one trusted that the fish or wildlife were safe to eat, not with chemicals leaching into everything. Skip must have been desperate when he decided to turn against his community.

Bumpass Cove asked the federal Environmental Protection Agency (EPA) to investigate the site. Hobert wrote to tell me about a meeting that he'd scheduled with them. I found out later that his wife, Gladys, had urged him to let Russell take the lead. She knew that Hobert's spirits were low after he found out about Skip. But Hobert said no, he had to finish this.

A week later Russell wrote to tell me they met the EPA on the landfill so Hobert could show them the site. They were with him when Hobert collapsed. He died a few days later.

My friend, my mentor was dead. I wept for days, letting the devastating news sink in. We suspected chemicals off-gassing and leaching from the landfill had played a role in his death.

At Hobert's funeral, his daughter grabbed my hand. "You're Miss Maury! My dad talked about you a whole lot. He sure liked you."

I hugged her as tears ran down my face. "I sure liked him too."

Hobert's death had motivated me to keep working with Bumpass Cove and the citizens across the state who were fighting chemical dumping. They were part of my life, my heart, and my new home in Tennessee.

When Hobert died, everything changed. He had been a man of few words who memorized the weak environmental laws Tennessee had on the books.

"The Tennessee Code Annotated says . . ." and he'd reel off a section of the state law that called hazardous waste "special waste."

"It's so special they want it buried alongside our kitchen waste. Mighty kind of them, don't y'all think?" Then, he would turn to gaze out at the creek that ran behind his house.

After I'd met Hobert, a spark surged inside me. The outside me looked the same—brown hair, blue eyes, glasses. When Hobert first shared his story about chemicals leaching from a nearby landfill into the pristine waters of Bumpass Cove creek, I got mad. How dare they? After that, each time I met a new challenge, that spark returned—and grew. When my phone was tapped by an anonymous opponent, more kindling was added to the fire. That flame intensified when the radio host called me a "Communist," during a live show, as if asking questions about pollution was taboo. When the flood mixed chemicals together causing an explosion, all hell broke loose. Then, Hobert had died.

After his death, I was a raging inferno. Grief and rage turned me into an incendiary device focused on stopping industry from contaminating more communities. No more people needed to get sick. Or die. I was committed to doing what I could to bring about justice.

seventeen

SLAYING DRAGONS

1980

I WAS DETERMINED to find out if there were more cases like Bumpass Cove. On one occasion, I drove from Brownsville to the town of Toone. It took less than an hour, but the heat and humidity baked me to the vinyl seat in my non-air-conditioned car. Sweat streamed down my face like a waterfall. A hot waterfall. But I was focused on who I was going to meet, not on the heat.

Nell Grantham had agreed to see me when I called her after reading an article about her in the local newspaper.

I asked, "Is this the woman who was written about in the paper? The one who's fighting chemical contamination from a local landfill?"

She replied. "Why, yes, I am. Who is calling, please?"

"I'm Maura Doherty. I work with a group of citizens who live near toxic waste sites."

We had a brief conversation and arranged to meet. Sticking to a car seat was a small price to find another ally against chemical dumping.

Meeting people I'd only read about in local newspapers didn't faze me anymore. Not since Hobert had died. Each day after I'd finished my job working with community clinics across Tennessee I'd head to the local library, which was where I found the article about Nell. A few lines said she'd criticized the government for not doing enough to protect Hardeman County citizens from chemicals that were coming from a nearby landfill. That was all I needed to open the local phone book to track her down.

⟡

AS I SAT with Nell Grantham and her sister, Janie, I sipped from a glass of sweet iced tea.

"How much do you know about what's going on here?" Nell leaned toward me across the oak dining table.

"Only what I read in the article."

Janie harrumphed and shook her head. "Oh, you poor girl. You don't know anything." Her blonde ponytail was pulled back so tightly I could see veins pulsating in her forehead.

Nell's eyes sought mine. She said, "It's high time someone took an interest in what's going on. The EPA says they've done everything they can. Velsicol just keeps dumping chemicals—mostly at night when no one's around. That site's filled with wildlife. Best fishing around. They only fenced off a small part where Velsicol dumped over a hundred thousand drums. Mostly pesticides. But lots of other companies brought their waste, too. The groundwater is contaminated. You can't tell me the fish and the deer and all those other critters aren't poisoned. We've lived here for decades, drinking the water, eating the fish. We're probably filled with toxins, too. The city took us off well water and put us on city water. But the chemicals are still there, leaching into everything." She lowered her head as if saying the words had beat her down.

Janie gripped her glass with both hands, fingers blanched white, like she was holding on for life.

I waited a few seconds. "Folks in Bumpass Cove in Upper East Tennessee are going through the same thing. Velsicol shipped waste to their sanitary landfill 500 miles from Memphis. They've had fish die, even explosions when the wrong chemicals mixed together."

Nell's cheeks flamed red, crimson spreading to her neck.

I nodded. "We're getting folks together to talk about their problems with chemical dumps. Do you want to join us?"

They looked at each other, then at me. In unison, they said, "Yes."

"I'll let you know when and where we're going to meet. Thanks for everything. And for the tea."

As I rose from my chair, Nell asked, "Have you heard about what's going on in Memphis? You might want to talk to them, too."

"Memphis?" I blinked.

Nell nodded. "Sounds like what's going on here and that place you talked about is happening there, too. You might want to include them."

◇

THE SHELBY COUNTY room of the Memphis Public Library held a treasure trove of newspapers dating back decades. The librarian's name—Edith—gleamed on a polished brass nametag on the shoulder of her pink sweater. Her drawl was almost a whisper as her slender finger traced the outline of several articles in the newspapers she'd selected.

"Oh, those poor people. We were just talking about them. North Hollywood area. Sounds like they're suffering something terrible. Let me know if I can help you with anything else." Her eyes sparkled as she patted the silver curls escaping from a recalcitrant bun on top of her head.

"Yes. Local phone books. Where might they be?"

Edith pointed to shelves a short distance away. "Good luck. Have a nice day."

By the time I'd finished, I'd found the names of two people fighting the Memphis landfill. I decided to find a motel, make calls, and meet them. The fire inside me raged hotter.

MRS. HARKINS BARELY filled the wingback chair in the church reception room. Reverend Green sat across from us. He spoke first.

"Miss Maura, we're so glad you've taken an interest in our cause. You say you're from Nashville?"

"Yes. I work for a nonprofit fighting chemical dumping. Part of my job was working in Kingsport in Upper East Tennessee. Their air smells like chemicals. The conference I coordinated brought a lot of people like you together. One group has a sanitary landfill chock full of chemicals. Many from Velsicol."

Mrs. Harkins shook her head. "We know Velsicol. Their pesticide manufacturing plant's not far from here."

Reverend Green leaned in closer. "That company, and others, have disposed of their waste in a landfill in our neighborhood. More trucks come every day, often at night. But we can't get anyone to listen to us. Folks are sick. Women are having miscarriages. Children can't concentrate in school. We don't know what to do."

"I'd like to help. The folks I work with want to meet others like you from around the state. We're going to host a meeting to bring us all together. Are you interested in joining us?"

"Oh, yes," he said.

"Yes, m'am, I'll be there," said Mrs. Harkins.

⋄

BY LATE 1979, when I wasn't working with clinics, I met with more people around the state who, like Bumpass Cove, Memphis, and Hardeman County, were worried about chemical contamination. I wrote to Russell to tell him what I'd learned and asked if he wanted to meet these folks. Using grant money left from the conference, Helen had arranged for all of us to meet.

A few months later, we sat at Highlander in the same familiar rocking chairs—Black and White folks, urban and rural, representing a cross section of citizens with a common goal: to protect their homes from chemical contamination. As they shared their stories, they discovered that Velsicol, the same company that had buried waste in Memphis and Hardeman County, had also dumped it in Bumpass Cove. That company had never imagined that people from one end of the state would talk to people from the other end about the poisons the company had dumped. That night the citizens decided to form a statewide group called Tennesseans Against Chemical Hazards, TEACH.

As I drove back to Nashville, I knew I had a decision to make. My job was working with community clinics, but my heart was with the folks fighting chemical contamination. When I got back to the office, I told Jonathan I was resigning to work full time for TEACH. After a long discussion, we worked out a plan for me to take a few months to finish up work on the clinic project. He agreed to let me keep an office at the center as long as I kept him and the Board of Directors updated.

At the next board meeting, I reported on the clinic project as well as TEACH.

David Wilson, a board member, spoke first. He had trained students in his chemistry class to test water quality across the state.

"Maura, tell us more about what's going on in Memphis."

I told him what I knew and, after the meeting, I gave him Reverend Green's and Mrs. Harkins' contact information.

He called me after he'd spoken with them. "They told me their neighbors have all sorts of illnesses. Their kids are always sick. Several women have had miscarriages, some of them multiple times. It's not right. My wife and I have been blessed with children. I need to see if there's anything I can do for them."

One weekend he drove to Memphis. When he got back, he called me. At first, I couldn't make out what he was saying. Mild-mannered David Wilson was shouting into the phone.

"Maura, this time I caught them red-handed. Those companies are going to burn for what they did!"

"David, what are you talking about? What did you find?"

"First of all, do you know there's not even a fence around that dumpsite? It might be 'closed,' but the children use it as a playground. Their pets walk across it and track all that mess back home."

"David, what mess?"

But he continued to rant, oblivious to my question, shouting so loudly that I had to pull the phone away from my ear.

"And you do you know how I found it?" he barked. "I stepped in it! A smelly mess sitting right there on the surface of the dump. Don't worry, I had on my rubber boots so I didn't spread it around."

I took a long breath. "What was it, David?"

"I took a sample, that's how I know. My GC-MS, you know, the gas chromatograph, mass spectrophotometer, did the magic. Three hundred thousand parts per million chlordane! One of the worst organochlorine insecticides Velsicol ever made. Sitting right there on the surface of the dump! No wonder those folks are sick. It off-gasses something awful. Smells nasty and is nasty. Toxic stuff. Now I have them."

"Wow!" I let the news sink in, scrambling to remember how toxic this pesticide was. "What should we do next?"

"What *should* we do? I already did it!"

Oh, Lord. He's a respected chemist from Vanderbilt University taking on Velsicol Chemicals. I know he wants to help but...

"Oh, Maura, don't you worry. All I did was call the EPA and tell them if they don't clean it up, I'll go public."

It took a few beats before I choked out, "What did they say?"

"Well, first they hemmed and hawed. Then I hung up on them."

"You what?" We needed his help, but this was moving a lot faster than I'd expected.

"They blinked first and called me back. We're meeting next weekend at the dumpsite. Maura, it's like Saint George slaying the dragon. Best of all, Velsicol can't do a thing to me. I've got tenure. They can't blast me out of here. This dragon is going to go down hard."

Saint George and David and the citizens across the state won the day. In time, the landfills in Memphis, Bumpass Cove, and Hardeman County were declared Superfund cleanup sites. That didn't mean that people hadn't been exposed or that the toxins were easily taken care of. But the sites would be evaluated and cleaned up as best as possible.

It took local citizens, one passionate Bronxite, and a dedicated chemist who put his foot in it to take those dragons down.

◇

WHEN I STARTED my job with TEACH, I had to meet with the representative of the New World Foundation. We needed a small grant to continue our work.

I greeted Gabe Mehrehteab at the Kingsport airport terminal. He shook my hand and said, "I need a beer."

Of all the things I planned to discuss with him, beer wasn't one of them. We had met one other time on a sweltering day in West Tennessee at the Rossville community clinic when sweat had streamed down his Black face as he looked out at the cotton fields and parched earth that surrounded us.

"Maura," he'd said then, "this is never-never land."

In spite of his discomfort at that first meeting, he was impressed with our work and recommended that the foundation approve funds to support the clinics across Tennessee. So maybe now a beer would help bring funding for TEACH as well.

"Gabe, Helen Lewis, and the others are waiting for us. How about we get a beer after the meeting?"

When I looked closer, his charcoal suit looked a bit rumpled from travel. Wrinkles around his deep brown eyes showed fatigue.

"No, Maura. I need a beer. Now."

I was his driver and contact person. If the man who funded TEACH and other projects wanted a beer, I should get him a beer. But where? I never drank in Kingsport. All the taverns looked boarded up to meet strict blue laws that required bars to prevent passersby from seeing inside. When we stepped outside the terminal, Kingsport's rancid air enveloped us.

"Maura, this smells very bad. What is that smell?" He pulled a white handkerchief from his pocket and pressed it to his nose.

"We say it smells like money, Gabe. Industry puts a lot of pollution into the air."

He muffled through the handkerchief, "I'll never complain about the air in Manhattan again."

As he placed his suitcase in the trunk of my car, I remembered seeing a sign for a new pub not far from our meeting across town.

I turned on the ignition and looked at him. "One beer and then we meet Helen."

He nodded. "Yes, Maura, one beer." With that he sat back and I drove to the pub.

A banner hung over a polished wooden door announcing: *The New Nickelodeon Pub*. Oak panels only half occluded the windows. I held my breath as we stepped inside—shiny wood floors, a gleaming mahogany bar, and track lighting overhead reassured me that this was a good choice. Several men sat at the bar and a group played pool in the back corner. Gabe took a seat at the bar while I headed to the restroom.

"You're with that Negro," a woman snarled at me as I entered the restroom, before she slammed me into the bathroom wall. She was about my height with bleached blonde hair; her hands had me pinned. I saw fury in her eyes. Hatred. Pure evil.

"Get off me," I yelled and, despite my shaky knees, I pushed her off. *Who in the hell is she?* I rammed past her and rushed out the door. I couldn't believe I'd been in a shoving match with a drunken bigot in a bathroom while Gabe was waiting for me.

He was sipping a beer, his charcoal suit and Black skin a stark contrast to the jeans and T-shirts on the White men playing pool in the corner.

"Gabe, let's get out of here," I said.

He turned to me.

"Now. Let's go." I placed quaking hands on the bar to steady myself.

"What's wrong?" he asked.

"Nothing, it's time. We need to meet the others. Let's leave." In no way did I want to delay our exit by telling him what had happened.

"Not yet." He took another sip, then slid something across the bar. "Look what I have."

It was a business card emblazoned with a red and black shield that proclaimed in big, bold letters, "Ku Klux Klan, Royal Order of Upper East Tennessee, Kingsport."

"Where did you get this?" My hand shook as I handed it back. *How far is the door? How fast can we get out of here?*

"Someone gave it to me. I think they are welcoming us." With that he drank more beer and turned to look over his shoulder.

Gabe was from Ethiopia. He had left home when a civil war broke out, finished college in the US, and took a job with the New World Foundation. Without his help, the money for TEACH and other projects would run out. I needed to get him out of there. Alive.

I told him about the woman in the bathroom and repeated, "We need to leave."

"Soon," he said, before he took another sip. "You need to know something about me." He lowered his glass. "I do not run away from a fight. In my country, we know how to fight." He wiped his mouth on a napkin, its red stars vibrant against a royal blue background.

I thought about the hatred that had pinned me to that wall. Then I made a decision. I pushed up Gabe's monogrammed sleeve and grabbed his wrist. "I need to get you out of here. Let's go."

Heavy footsteps thudded behind us. A six-foot-something pool player landed his cue stick with a whack on the floor.

"Y'all better get out of here if you know what's good for y'all." He kept his voice low, but his meaning was clear.

I tightened my grip on Gabe's wrist as the man continued. "Y'all are not welcome here."

As I gazed past our visitor; the woman from the bathroom came toward us with several more men.

"Now, Gabe," I said, between clenched teeth.

"Oh," he said, turning to face the man behind us.

Our visitor's mustache twitched as Gabe said, "We will leave."

The man started to walk away.

"When I finish my beer."

With that the man turned back to us as the others joined him.

Gabe drained his glass, placed it on the bar, and stood up. "Well, Maura, we do have other places to go, don't we?" He beamed a smile around the now silent bar, pulled down his cuffs, brushed off his sleeves, and gestured toward the door. "Shall we?"

Once we got into the car and locked the doors, my whole body vibrated as I struggled to get the key in the ignition.

He asked, "Are you all right?"

"I will be, Gabe. But how are you?" When I finally was able to pull out of the parking space, my heart was pounding. I eyed the rearview mirror to make sure no one had followed us.

"Oh, I am fine. I cannot wait to tell my friends in New York about the very exciting place you brought me to, this Kingsport. Do not worry. It tells me that we need this work of yours more than ever. You will get your funding."

I drove to the meeting with my body still quaking. Seeing Helen and our colleagues helped still my nerves, but it wasn't until I took my friend and coworker Jamie Cohen aside and told her what had happened that I felt some relief.

Home seemed very far away.

◆

FRIENDS LIKE JAMIE opened doors for me. A power-packed, five feet one, Jamie's insight and work ethic radiated as she championed worker safety initiatives while I focused on

TEACH. Our work was nonstop and, if we were lucky, we'd meet in Nashville between trips across the state. One evening as we sat on her porch swing, eyes closed, exhausted from late nights and long drives, Jamie leapt off the swing and shouted.

"Maura, we need a vacation. I need one, you need one. Let's blow this pop stand."

I knew she was right. "But what about Jonathan? He'll never go for it." He was unhappy I was leaving the clinic job and needed me to write the annual report for the clinic project before I worked for TEACH.

"You leave him to me, Maura. Go home and get ready. I'll pick you up in a few hours." We slid off the swing and went to pack. I didn't ask where we were going. I trusted her and knew we could only afford a short getaway on our tight budget. After I stowed my backpack in her trunk, we drove past Nashville's replica of the Parthenon that stood in the middle of Centennial Park. Quite a send-off for our next adventure.

"We'll spend tonight with my parents in Arkansas. They're in Blytheville where I grew up. I can't wait for you to meet them. From there we should head to New Orleans, don't you agree?"

I didn't say, "Arkansas? New Orleans? Aren't they in opposite directions?" Instead, I said, "Sounds great!"

She and I had spent hours crisscrossing the South as if our cars were more than a lowly Pinto and a Datsun. Driving across more state lines didn't sound very different than what we did every day, except now we'd be on vacation and we'd be driving together.

I gazed out at the rolling hills that bordered Tennessee and said, "Jamie, I miss Hobert," and blinked back tears. His death had created an overwhelming sense of purpose over everything I did. And I knew he'd like that I was taking a vacation to keep my energy going for the work ahead.

Jamie reached over and held my hand as we traveled down that road, carrying Hobert's memory with us. I didn't ask what she'd said to Jonathan that convinced him we needed a break, but I found out when we pulled into her parents' driveway. Her mother and father came out to greet us. After they'd hugged and Jamie introduced me, her mother said, "There's a phone message for Maura from Jonathan in Nashville."

Jamie shrugged and we went inside to stash our bags. I found the phone and turned to her. "Jamie, what exactly did you say to Jonathan before we left?"

"I put a note on his desk, Maura. He'd already left the office."

I gulped, knowing what was going to unfold. Jamie was Jonathan's friend. She'd worked with him for years as an undergrad and now on occupational health. Me? After the extra months it had taken to pull off the Kingsport conference, he'd kept his distance. A few months before the conference he'd even told the Board of Directors a lie about me stealing money from the project.

When I'd heard about it, I confronted him.

"Jonathan, why did you tell the board that I stole money?"

He stared at me.

"Do you have any proof that I stole money?" I hissed.

He looked down at his desk before he looked up and shook his head. "No."

My voice dropped to almost a whisper. "How dare you lie about me. My name is Maura Bridget Clare Doherty, and I don't steal. You will call another meeting of the board to tell them you were wrong and to apologize to me. In public."

He did. After that, the gulf between us widened. The *NO* that had reverberated in my head when I'd first shaken his hand had warned me not to trust him. And it had been right.

It didn't surprise me that, when he answered the phone, he shouted so loudly Jamie heard him from across the room. All I could say was "Yes, Jonathan," before he bellowed more. "I didn't know that a grant was due. Don't worry, I'll get it done." I reassured him that we'd only be away for a few days but that didn't appease him. By the time the call ended, Jamie looked to be in shock. She hadn't understood how difficult things were between him and me.

"Jamie, it's just how it is. When we get back, I'll get the grant written and he'll calm down." I knew that was only partly true. I had memories of Sister Christine throwing down the keys to the trunk room and screaming as I quaked in my seat. There was definitely something wrong with Jonathan, but it wasn't mine to figure out.

Jamie and I got up early the next morning and drove south, following the Mississippi River toward New Orleans. Wide riverbanks stretched into deltas that hosted cypress and oak. The occasional swamp disappeared from view as we drove several more hours through Mississippi into Louisiana where the air was thick with jasmine. When we arrived, we dropped our bags at her friend's condo, then headed on foot to Jackson Square. As we got closer, we had to push our way past throngs of people singing, yelling, and drinking from plastic cups decorated with little umbrellas. Zydeco music poured out of open doorways.

"Welcome to New Orleans, Maura. It's time to relax and have fun." By the time we made it to the square, I felt like

I'd been transported to another planet. A man in tails and top hat rode by on a unicycle while juggling colorful balls. A woman sat on the corner with a crystal ball offering psychic readings. There were so many performers I couldn't keep track of them all as we made our way to Café du Monde where Jamie introduced me to beignets and chicory coffee. She blew powdered sugar at me from the top of her beignet. "It brings good luck," she said.

We bought balloons from a man who looked like Danny DeVito. His sign proclaimed that he was Nick, the Italian Stallion. His friend Ted played guitar from his wheelchair a few yards away, singing about a clock in a tower going ". . . tick, tock, tick, tock."

We spent time with them between our walks down side streets where we admired the ornate ironwork of the French Quarter. That evening, Nick invited us to picnic on a beach outside town. After they packed up their gear, Nick opened the van's side door, pulled out a ramp, and pushed the wheelchair inside. Jamie and I slid onto a bench seat, clicking on seat belts. I didn't worry about getting into a vehicle with two strange men. There was something about this trip and these men that lightened my fears.

Several minutes later, Nick pulled into a small parking lot, lowered the ramp, and wheeled Ted out, guitar and all. We sat on a blanket close to the walkway that looked out over the Gulf of Mexico. Sultry air washed over us. When I dipped my toes in the water, I was shocked at how warm it was, unlike the bracing cold of the Atlantic Ocean of my childhood. Darkness enveloped me as I laid back on the blanket to see a star-studded sky. It reminded me how vast the universe was, and how all I had to do was look up to remember. We ate and drank and laughed about the tangled threads that had brought us together.

"Me, I got here by running away from my wife and children," Nick said as we gazed at the moon's reflection on the water. "Suburban New Jersey wasn't for me. I felt like I was dying with the corporate job, the endless need to work and work. I left it all, bought the panel truck, and here I am with you and with my buddy Ted."

I was shocked that he'd abandoned his family. Then I thought, *I left God and my Sister community behind. Were we really that different?*

Ted slung his guitar strap over his shoulder and sang his clock song. After the last chord echoed around us, he told us where his inspiration had come from. "I was in law school and the stress about killed me. I decided to end it all, so I jumped off the tower on Tulane's campus." He paused, his words drifting into the night as I held back tears. "Funny thing. Instead of dying, I landed in this wheelchair singing about the clock up in that tower." His long blonde hair caught the moonlight as he sang another song.

A few days later, we said goodbye and returned home, the aroma of jasmine surrounding us as we drove. I spent several days and nights writing the grant proposal. Every so often, I looked up and thought about Nick and Ted and that star-studded sky. And how those men had escaped lives that were dragging them down. I thought back to my pain of leaving the convent to get away from a life that had been choking me, how stress had strangled my muscles until it was hard to breathe.

I had no idea that in another year stress would trigger a major health crisis for me, and that depression would haunt me years later. Or how, even with my work in Tennessee, my dreams still included the swish of long habits and the click of rosary beads. I wondered if Nick and Ted dreamed about their former lives as well. I only knew that each of us had done what we'd needed to do to save ourselves, despite how much pain it caused. Maybe, more than our differences, we had that in common.

And there was Jamie, who shared my passion for justice, for helping others, who believed in taking time out to restore her spirits. She helped me see the similarities in the people around me and to notice the stars overhead.

✧

MY WORK IN Tennessee taught me a lot about chemical pollution, but I wanted to know more. I applied to environmental programs at several schools of public health, hoping it would help fill in the gaps in my knowledge. I thought back to how my father had wanted to go to college, and here I was looking to get into my second graduate school. I think he'd be proud of me. But after I was accepted into the University of California at Berkeley, I was torn. How could I leave Tennessee and the amazing people who had been home for me over the past few years? And to go to Berkeley, of all places, where the convent had offered to send me to finish my undergraduate degree. I hadn't been ready then. Was I ready now?

What would Hobert say? I cried, then laughed, and imagined him saying, "Go on, Maury. Learn more and help others."

I was ready. I let each of the community groups know I'd be leaving at the end of the summer. At my last TEACH meeting, Russell Rogers stood up and raised his hand.

"Maura, I have somethin' for you from all of us. This here comes from our heart to thank you for everythin' you did to help us. Not just us folks in Bumpass Cove but in all of Tennessee." With that he handed me a package, sat down and wiped tears from his face. His wife, Mary Lee, patted his arm and smiled at me.

I broke down in tears, and everyone laughed and cried until Nell called out, "Open it, open it," and they all cheered.

I unwrapped the first gift to find a plaque inscribed with all their names.

"Read it to us, Maura." Russell prompted.

I cleared my throat and began. "Appreciation Award to Maura Doherty, with deep appreciation for the faithful and devoted services you have given us." As I finished reading the plaque, more tears rolled down my face.

"Come on, now," Nell from Hardeman County urged. "There's one more."

The next one took my breath away. It was a cardboard cutout of Wonder Woman with my name at the bottom signed by all the members. Her magic lasso hung from her waist ready to find the truth in the next situation.

"Maura, you've been our Wonder Woman. And we can't thank you enough." Russell came over, hugged me, and everyone joined in.

That night as I lay in bed, I gazed at the plaque and the figure of Wonder Woman. After Highlander, Hobert, and TEACH became part of my life, Tennessee had become home for me. How could I leave these dear friends who were like family to me?

And would I ever find home again?

⋄

THE DAY I left Nashville for Berkeley, I stopped to pick up my last paycheck. Cathy, the bookkeeper, who had been one of the first to welcome me to the Center, told me, "I don't have it. Jonathan told me to send it back to the bursar's office. He said it was made out for too much money." Her red hair seemed to curl even tighter as she stared at me.

I leaned in close. "Cathy, you know he's wrong. You get that check back within the hour. When I get it, I'm leaving for California."

I barely earned enough to put gas in my car and pay rent with two other roommates. Cathy was one of those roommates. She should have had my back. I walked around campus to cool off, went back to the office, picked up the check, cashed it, and drove off.

What was wrong with Jonathan? Why hadn't Cathy, Jamie, and my other allies at the Center believed me when I told them the things Jonathan had done to me? As I left town, I put it all out of my mind. He wasn't my problem anymore. I was off to my next adventure.

A decade later, I received an invitation to attend the center's 25th anniversary. I wasn't sure I wanted to go. Did I want to go back? Jonathan was no longer there and my colleague Barb was the director. She was doing stellar work in maternal and infant care around the state. The celebration would be for the community clinics I had worked with. I decided to go.

I loved reconnecting with everyone. We toasted community leaders who had dedicated themselves to supporting community health over many decades. I was thrilled to have played a small role in supporting them. During the picnic on the lawn, Cathy, the former bookkeeper, came up to me, tears running down her face.

"Maura, I'm so sorry."

"Cathy, what's wrong. Are you okay?" I had no idea why she was apologizing. I had left it all behind a long time ago.

"I didn't believe you. We, your friends, none of us believed you. About Jonathan. I had no idea you were right."

It all came back to me. His anger, his abusive behavior toward me. How I'd steel myself to talk with him. How I had to fight him every time he lied or berated me. How he tried to deprive me of my last paycheck. How none of my female coworkers seemed to see his dark side. "Cathy, that's all in the past. It's all right. Don't worry."

She rubbed her tears with a jerk of her fingers as if she was flicking off dirt. "You don't know. You don't know."

Now I was at a loss. "Don't know what?"

"After he left the center, we found out he had affairs with his female students. None of us knew. One of the women . . ." With this she took a ragged breath as more tears flowed. ". . . she needed professional help. There's probably more we'll never know about."

I leaned in and hugged her. How sad. It sounded as if Jonathan had mistreated other women. We stood there for several minutes as others laughed and strummed guitars while the aroma of magnolias permeated the air. "Cathy, I'm glad you told me." I sat with her on the porch swing as the sunset lit up the sky in magenta and orange.

Decades later, with the emergence of the "Me Too," movement, I thought about Jonathan. I was grateful I'd had the confidence to fight back. And that he hadn't been successful in sabotaging my work.

I send healing thoughts to his victims and all the women who have been abused by men in power.

part four

Stories, Not Secrets

CELTIC TREE OF LIFE

eighteen

I DIDN'T HAVE A SEIZURE

IN 1981, ON my first day at the University of California's School of Public Health in Berkeley, I reminded myself, *I'm here to learn so I can help others*. My heart raced as I sat, pen poised, notebook open, waiting for the toxicology professor to begin his lecture.

Professor Benjamin took his place behind the lectern, black hair shining, his eyes looking intent behind rimless glasses as he gazed at the sea of first-year graduate students. "Chemicals don't kill people."

The rest of his remarks were a blur. *Had he really said that?* I thought of Hobert, dead from what I'd assumed was toxic chemicals.

"Show me the dead bodies. Who has seen dead bodies from chemical exposure?"

No one moved. The student next to me looked at his notebook. The woman across from me studied her nails. My arm inched upwards until my hand was high in the air.

"You. Where did you see dead bodies?" He glared at me as if I'd defied him.

"Tennessee."

"Oh." He swatted toward me with the wave of a hand. "That happens there. It does not happen here."

My head pounded. How could I have left my allies in Tennessee only to be told that chemicals didn't kill people? Had I been I wrong to come here, to pack up my life in the hope of helping others fight chemical contamination?

On my last trip to Bumpass Cove, Russell Rogers had hugged me, and said, "Go out there to California, learn everything, and help others. Promise?"

"Promise."

Now, my hope was being crushed by the very expert we needed in our fight against chemical dumping. To his credit, the professor continued to lecture on how certain doses were needed before they damaged health. However, nothing he said put me at ease. And when I left the class, my fellow students walked the other way.

I went back to my room and cried. *Hobert, what have I done?*

Luckily, over time, I found a few students who understood how chemical contamination could damage health. In addition, my part-time job at a nonprofit allowed me to research pesticides. I found out about similar patterns in California where pesticide disposal problems were just surfacing.

By then I was in a relationship with K.W. from Portland, Oregon. My friend, Thalia, had introduced him to me early that summer. I was captivated by his sweet drawl. He and I called each other several times a week and flew back and forth to see each other. My life was full. The stress of keeping school, work, and my personal life in balance was daunting. It came to a head in the course called biostatistics. When I tried to apply "f" values, probability, and confidence intervals to textbook examples, I floundered. After I failed the first midterm, I panicked. Keeping the fellowship that paid my tuition depended me on maintaining a B average. Instead of keeping my struggle to myself, I spoke to my co-worker at the pesticide project.

"Mary, I just failed my statistics midterm. I don't know what to do. I'm lost."

She looked at me. "Did you know that I'm in the doctoral program in biostatistics? Why don't I help you?"

It was as if floodgates had opened and hope rushed in. I fell into her arms. This usually low-key woman who shared a workspace with me took it in stride and held me close.

"Yes," I said. "I need your help."

I spent weeks with Mary studying statistical concepts followed by hours to complete the rest of my coursework. I didn't tell her about my midnight hits of E&J brandy that helped provide some relief from the endless hours of study. I brought my failing grade up to a B. Year one of the two-year program ended in a celebration of beer and brandy with friends.

But the fear of failure and the stressful year had taken its toll on me. At the end of that year, I was bone-tired. Nothing I did, no amount of sleep, not even being excited about spending the summer with K.W., seemed to help. He'd flown to Berkeley so we could drive back to Portland together,

I told him, "Something's wrong with me but I don't know what." My plan was to live with him in Portland while I completed an internship with the Oregon Department of Environmental Quality, DEQ.

I looked out the window as we drove over the Golden

Gate Bridge and thought, *just relax. It's summer. You finished one year of the two-year graduate program. Take it easy.*

But my body didn't know what that meant.

⟡

ONE NIGHT, SOON after I arrived in Portland, I was jolted from sleep.

"Maura. Maura. Wake up." A stranger in a white uniform leaned over me calling my name.

The overhead light glared as I struggled to open my eyes. When I managed to force them open, I saw K.W. sitting next to me in bed, crying. The stranger in a white suit sat on the other side of me. I couldn't move my mouth. It was as if every muscle in my face had frozen in place. It was way worse than the muscle spasms I'd endured in the past. When I tried to move my arms, I couldn't. They seemed paralyzed. Finally, I looked at the man in white and croaked out, "Who . . . the . . . hell . . . are . . . you?"

The man in white laughed as K.W. choked out, between sobs, "He's an EMT, Maura. You had some kind of seizure. I called 9-1-1 for an ambulance."

Even with all my muscles aching, I slurred, "I . . . didn't . . . have . . . a . . . seizure."

So began months of medical exams to determine the cause of the very real grand mal seizure that had hit me in my sleep. That month I saw a neurologist who was the first of several to agree on a diagnosis.

"You have epilepsy and will need to be on medication for the rest of your life." He added that after the age of thirty, medication was essential to control seizures.

I was thirty-three. Why had this happened? How would I finish graduate school and pay for medications? I spent sleepless nights worried about having another seizure. I needed help. I didn't want to risk another episode that might kill off more brain cells. What if I kept having seizures and couldn't get my degree or hold down a job? I promised the doctor I'd start medication as soon as I returned to campus where I had medical insurance. I had another incentive—they had revoked my driver's license until I submitted a doctor's note that my seizures were controlled by medication. I finished the internship at DEQ, left my car with K.W., went back to California, found another neurologist, and started medication. My car stayed with K.W. until I moved back to Portland after graduation.

1982—my final year of graduate school. Enter Maura, drugged on phenobarbital, a barbiturate, looking like the strung-out hippies who slept in doorways on Telegraph Avenue. I could barely function. I sleepwalked to the bus, got off at school, and walked onto campus in a daze.

"Maura, are you all right?" my academic advisor asked as he passed me in the hall.

I turned around and stared at him for a few seconds before I remembered who he was.

"No," I said. "I'm not okay." I kept walking, trying to remember where my next class was. I imagine he let my other professors know I was going through a crisis.

I didn't care who knew. I didn't even care that I couldn't drive. Mass transit and my bicycle gave me easy access to campus. What mattered was that I couldn't think. The courses in Industrial Hygiene were a blur, and the labs that went along with them were impenetrable. I asked several classmates for help but they refused to lend me their notes so I could catch up on the classes I'd missed. Each one said, "I never lend out my notes."

Were they afraid I might do better than them on upcoming tests? I'll never know. The good thing about being stoned on drugs was that I didn't care. By the time the third student refused to help me, I knew I needed a new strategy. And there it was, listed in the course catalog. "INC." I could take an incomplete in the course I was failing so I could end the year with a passing grade. Solution found. I filed for an incomplete as my body flashed into a fever and broke out in hives—side effects from the medication.

My doctor was matter-of-fact. "It happens. Let's get you off phenobarb, wait a few days, and start you on another medication."

Enter Dilantin and its effects that included mood changes, panic attacks, trouble sleeping, and agitation. I took a break from school, letting them know I had a seizure disorder. Within days my body rejected the new medication with a repeat cycle of fever and hives.

I called K.W. "I'm going to stop taking medication."

I heard panic in his voice. "Maura, if the doctor says you need to take it, you should take it."

"None of these meds agree with me. I need to get them out of my system and see how I feel."

I went back to the neurologist who had yet a third prescription called Tegretol ready for me. "Tell me about the possible side effects."

He picked up his reading glasses and scanned the Physician's Desk Reference. "Risk of seizures, skin rashes . . ."

"No."

"What?" he asked. "What do you mean, no?"

"No more drugs. I think my seizure was caused by stress. I've lightened my course load and cut back on work to balance my schedule. Once I get over these hives and night sweats, I think I'll be myself again. I'll wait and see what happens but until then, no more medication."

With this he slammed the book closed. "You're going to die without medication. Don't even try it."

I stared at him and realized that, even though he was supposed to look out for me, he had a nasty way of showing it.

I lowered my voice. "Doctor, it's my decision."

As I left his office, I heard him yelling, "You're going to fall off your bicycle and get hit by a bus."

With that, I got on my bike, rode home, and didn't get hit by a bus.

LUCKY FOR ME, I was right. Once the medication left my system, my symptoms resolved. I slept through the night and could think clearly enough to finish my course assignments, keeping a B average with no more seizures. Doing what the doctor said, taking medication, was not the right thing for me. Breaking the rule to follow the doctor's advice, and paying attention to my instincts was what I needed to do.

The final hurdle was to take an oral exam before a panel of professors so I could graduate with a master's degree in public health.

My fellow students took No-Doz and rode the anxiety wave to cram for finals and orals. I didn't have that luxury. The seizure had killed enough brain cells so I studied as best as I could and slept through the night. Optimistic me, awake and alert, walked into the oral exam, happy to have passed the coursework. A half dozen male professors sat behind the table.

I don't remember the questions. I do remember trying to answer as I clenched sweaty palms in my lap. At one point, the professor who taught the course I had dropped, stood up and yelled, "You're so stupid. I don't even know why you're here."

Everyone froze. The other professors stared at him. My advisor was stunned, his mouth open in shock.

After more silence, I asked my advisor, "Would you please help out here?"

He stood up and led the huffing and puffing professor out of the room. Neither of them returned.

"Now, where were we?" I asked. My calm voice did not reveal my panic. I had to finish this. They had to finish this. My hands were still clenched in my lap.

Sometimes we meet our enemy, and it is us. It might have been my laid-back approach that slowed my answers to incoherence. I'll never know. As humiliated as I was at the professor's outburst, I knew I needed to get out of there as fast as possible. They gave me a passing grade. I graduated, packed my bags, and moved in with K.W. in Portland.

A few years later, during a professional conference, the school's administrative assistant took me aside. "I heard what our professor did to you during orals."

It was 1991. I was a Certified Industrial Hygienist (CIH) who specialized in worker safety. With these words my face flamed hot with shame as I remembered the humiliation of that day eight years ago. I shook my head. "I don't know what that was about."

"He was pretty messed up. We'd all heard about your seizure. His daughter had a seizure disorder, and he took his anxiety out on you. I'm sorry you had to bear the brunt of it."

I nodded, thanked her for checking in, and went back

to the conference. I wish I could say I went home, had a good career, and everything turned out just fine. But it didn't quite work out that easily. The fear and anxiety that I carried with me, the part of me that had surged into a full blown grand mal seizure, was still inside me, waiting to re-emerge. Drinking alcohol became my way to keep the fear down as I made a new life in Portland.

No Wonder Woman, magic lasso, or miracle drug would fix it.

◆

"I NEED TO sleep," I muttered, eyes half open, as I pulled into the Quik-Stop down the road from the refinery in the state of Washington's Puget Sound. I had been working in the safety profession for eight years and had just finished a graveyard shift evaluating toxic hazards for employees. Work now focused on protecting workers. K.W. and I had ended our relationship, so living away from Portland was a good option. Beautiful Birch Bay was a short drive from the condo my employer had rented for me.

As I dragged myself out of the car, I wondered if this job was my reward for years of study—working through the night pulling samples from refinery towers to test for leftover chemicals. Then struggling to sleep the day away so I could do it all over again. Beer was the answer. When my shift ended at 6:00 a.m., I bought a few stale sandwiches and a six-pack of Budweiser. Work, eat, drink, sleep, repeat. My own personal *Groundhog Day* without Bill Murray to keep me company.

To prove that the tanks were safe to enter, I had to climb ladders that hugged the sides of twelve-story towers, taking samples on each level. During a typical day, the towers had held crude oil or other petroleum products, but the towers had been emptied and ventilated so we safety specialists could take samples to verify that the air inside was safe to breathe. If the air met the criteria, contractors could go in and clean the inside of the tanks.

When my shift started, I climbed a ladder to the top hatch and attached a glass sample container to a pump that pulled air from inside the tower into the container. A telescoping painter's pole extended the sample bottle six feet or so inside the tower to get the best sample of what the workers might breathe. I'd pull the sample bottle back in, secure it in bubble wrap, stow everything in my backpack, and climb down to the next opening until I reached the ground. Then I'd walk the samples to the mobile lab before moving on to the next tower.

My first climb up was harrowing.

Dave, the lead, had told me, "Don't look down. Just climb up, and when you get to the top, look straight out. Don't . . . look . . . down."

I did what he said. Coveralled in fluorescent yellow Nomex with heavy-duty work gloves, steel-toed boots, hard hat, and safety glasses, I put one foot in front of the other and went up the ladder. On the first catwalk, I cinched the backpack tighter, gripped the next set of handrails, and climbed to the next level and the next and the next until I reached the top. In spite of the tank being shut down, the air was rank with petrochemicals.

Don't look down. Look straight out. My heart thrummed like a drum as sweat poured into my gloves. I forced my breath in and out, reminding myself that the tower had a sturdy catwalk. Once I no longer felt faint, I looked and there it was—the refinery bathed in a halo of lights that outlined every tower and process vessel against a black sky. It looked like an industrial Disneyland, only without Minnie or Mickey to share the magic. To the west lay Puget Sound and Birch Bay, wreathed in night and fog and wonder.

I can do this. I need this job.

I turned, unpacked my gear, and started sampling. The sound I feared the most was the crack of a sample container breaking inside my pack. It had happened several times before I mastered the art of securing bubble wrap around each glass tube.

Drinking beer after each shift didn't lessen my anxiety at climbing towers, but it was my security blanket. It gave me the illusion of relaxation and kept my fear in check, at least for a few hours. But my anxiety escalated each time I climbed and looked straight out like I'd been told, only to find my heart pounding and hands sweating so much the gloves slipped around as if they were sizes too big. I hadn't known I was afraid of heights. But I'd never climbed a hydrocracker tower before. Even with a graduate degree from Berkeley and a national board certification in Industrial Hygiene, I quaked in my boots. I was so lightheaded I had to take several deep breaths, pretending that the lights surrounding me were part of a new wonderland. I needed to combat my fear of heights to prove I was ready for full-time work with the consulting company that had hired me.

Don't look down.

Weeks went by. Each shift I managed to climb the towers and take the needed samples, After each shift I drank enough beer so I could sleep a few hours and go back to work.

Then I got to know Carl, the late-shift operations manager.

"Ops 1 to Safety 1. Come in, Safety 1." The radio call came in at 3:00 a.m., after I'd dropped off another round of samples.

"Safety 1. Come in, Ops 1."

"Safety needed in the Ops office ASAP."

"Ten four, Ops 1. On my way."

What would merit a call to me at three in the morning? Worst case scenario, an explosion or fire. Everything on site was flammable and explosive. But I'd heard nothing out of the ordinary over the radio in the last few hours. Alarms would have sounded, and an evacuation would have been ordered. Maybe it was something I did. Or didn't do.

By the time I'd made it to Carl's office, I was out of guesses. He stood with his back to me, working with something on the counter.

"I have a question for you, Safety Maura." He turned around with a stainless-steel cup in his hand. "Would you prefer a cappuccino or latte?" He laughed and stepped away to reveal a state-of-the-art espresso machine waiting for my order.

Cappuccino breaks at 3:00 a.m. became another lifeline that pulled me through. But none of it felt like home.

◇

AFTER I FINISHED the job at the petroleum refinery, I took a trip to Maui to visit my friend Jodi. That's where I learned something important—don't scuba dive with a hangover. Years earlier Jodi and I had paddled in Baja in a double Klepper kayak around the Sea of Cortez. She steered the rudder with foot pedals, and we glided past pelicans diving into azure water to feast on unlucky fish. We bonded over luscious meals cooked over wood fires, gazed in wonder at bioluminescence on the night tide, and slept under a million stars. She invited me to visit her in Maui, an island I hadn't yet explored. I booked a trip there a few months later.

Maui was filled with lush tropical forests and idyllic beaches. Jodi and I sat on her lanai and drank wine while we were serenaded by the calls of wild birds and surrounded by a fragrance of plumeria. As we finished our second bottle, she looked at me from her chaise lounge, short black hair gelled into daring spikes.

"I promised my friend Glenn we'd go see him. Is that all right with you?"

"Of course." I admired the ruby red bougainvillea wrapped around the open-air patio.

She drove toward the ocean and pulled up to a house that was half hidden behind a grove of palm trees. We got out and she tapped a French-manicured nail on the slatted screen that served as a front door. "Glenn. We're here."

A voice floated out from inside the house. "Come on in, honey."

I followed her past rattan chairs, jute rugs, and elaborate wooden carvings onto the lanai at the back of the house. A man in a Panama shirt and chino shorts lay on a lounger at the far end, his bronze tan a stark contrast to a bone-white shirt. He pushed his sunglasses to the tip of his nose and eyed me. "Well, who do we have here, Jodi?" His blue eyes were as clear as the ocean that pounded outside.

"Glenn, this is Maura, the woman I met kayaking in Baja. She's from Portland."

He reached out a hand that grasped mine like iron. "Welcome, Maura. Any friend of Jodi and all that. Would you like some wine?"

The rest of the day was filled with red wine and appetizers, including a sticky white paste called poi. Glenn said its sweetness would turn sour as it aged. The fiery glow of sunset tinted the lanai a light rosy-pink. I don't remember getting back to Jodi's or setting the alarm so I'd make the scuba diving trip I booked for the next day. When the alarm sounded, it cut through the fuzziness in my head before I washed my face and brushed my teeth. I tiptoed out while Jodi was still asleep and made it to the dock in time to don my shortie wet suit and collect my gear. My head pounded and my stomach protested. The blanks on the registration form wavered before my eyes.

Get a grip. Maura. You'll be okay.

Several others gathered around, full of chatter about dive conditions here and around the world. The couple next to me were from Kansas. I think they said Kansas.

"I'm Keith. She's Shelly. We don't have an ocean where we hail from." He pointed to himself and the woman next to him. His neon red wetsuit accentuated his paunch like an appendage.

When Shelly shook my hand, it dripped sweat. "This is so exciting. It's our first dive after we got certified. Are you nervous too?"

I nodded but knew nerves weren't my problem—it was having drunk wine into the wee hours of the morning. I cinched the buoyancy vest around me, gathered my mask, and snorkel, and moved away from Keith's booming laugh that pounded nails into my head. It never occurred to me to cancel the dive. It had been a several hours since my last glass of wine and I'd loved all the dive trips I'd taken before.

I'll be fine.

The fresh air soothed me as the boat made its way to the dive spot, the sun beaming full force overhead. The coastline faded from view as we pulled up to a coral reef off the coast of Molokai. Terry, the divemaster, and her assistant, Robin, circled among us as we inspected scuba tanks and regulators. When everyone was ready, we buddied up. I partnered with Dixie, an airline attendant from Dallas. Her blonde hair matched accents slashed across her turquoise wet suit.

"Pleased to meet you, Maura." Her voice sparked with excitement.

We role-played the signals we'd use to check on each other—thumbs up if everything was okay, thumbs down if it wasn't, and one hand choking the neck to show the low air alarm was going off. If anyone's alarm sounded or gave a thumbs down, everyone had to return to the boat. Dixie and I helped each other don tanks, recheck gauges, and insert mouthpieces. Then, one after another, we jumped in the water.

We met up about ten feet below the surface. Terry and Robin checked there were thumbs up all around. Save for the sound of air bubbles from my exhaled breath, it was silent. We were surrounded by schools of tropical fish decked out in garish colors including Moorish idols, their yellow and black stripes glowing in the sunlight that penetrated the water.

See, Maura? You're okay.

Even hungover I was mesmerized. I was floating in the ocean just a few feet from Dixie, whose hair surrounded her like a new species of kelp.

When Terry gave the signal, we deflated our buoyancy

vests to go deeper, air bubbles tracking our descent. We swam toward the coral reef as a seahorse three inches long swam by. It curled its tiny body to propel itself as it moved past. Lime green fish with purple polka dots swirled around me; I floated as a school of tang surrounded me, neon yellow pulsing against the white coral.

Time stopped—until my hangover reminded me it was still there, and vomit rose up in my throat threatening to choke me.

I could die down here.

Dixie was a few feet away looking at the coral as I struggled to swallow.

No. Don't let this happen.

I don't know how, but a few minutes later as I hovered over the coral, my symptoms eased. Dixie looked up, motioned for me to join her, and I swam over. I took one slow breath at a time, through the regulator, bubbles rising, waiting to see if the episode was over, wondering if I would die there on the coral reef. I fought the urge to give a thumbs down. I didn't want to cut the dive short for everyone.

Robin joined us and signaled us to another section of coral. After she held up her hand asking us to pause, she moved her hand toward the mouth of a small opening. She opened and closed her hand like a set of jaws in front of the opening. A moray eel with black and white dots poked its head out and opened and closed its mouth in rhythm with her hand. Robin moved closer and stroked the top of the eel's head, once, twice. She was petting it! I was amazed. The eel was placid, as if it accepted the intrusion as an everyday occurrence. Robin withdrew her hand and motioned me to take her place. I mimicked her, opening and closing my hand a few inches from the eel, and it mirrored me, breathing in and out as its jaws opened and closed. I stroked its head, its skin softer than I expected. Breathing in, out, my head began to clear, and my stomach settled.

As I watched Dixie pet the eel, I felt at peace. Even though the decision to scuba dive was risky given how hungover I was, I'd learned something—I couldn't hide from reality even on the ocean floor. The eel's breathing, in and out, struck a chord with me. The simplicity and beauty of this underwater world told me something about myself.

Drinking was getting in the way of my life.

And if I didn't stop drinking, I would die.

◇

SOON AFTER THE Maui trip, I flew back to our home in the Bronx. I hadn't been there for six months. But this trip was different—Mom was dying. As I sat at the kitchen table, M&Ms were my lifeline. I grabbed a handful and shoved them in my mouth. On the flight to New York, I promised myself I wouldn't drink. I was afraid if I started, I wouldn't be able to stop. The slow surge of sugar from the candy lubricated me. I hadn't slept for days, awash in an aching hollow of fear as my mother lay dying in the girls' bedroom. She was so quiet she was almost gone. But not yet. No moans, just the slow in and out of breath. Hunched over the bag of M&Ms, all I could do was sit at the kitchen table and eat. I pushed the grief away and attempted to write a safety training program for nameless, faceless workers who needed protection on the job. But I needed protection, too. From death. From this house that had brought me to life with six siblings. From parents who never told their stories. I grabbed another fistful of candy and pushed it into my mouth as if my life depended on it.

And, in a way, it did.

Over the past few years, alcohol had filled the hole inside me, the chasm that none of my friends knew about, the one that told me that I wasn't good enough, that I would fail at my job and at relationships. It had taken decades for me to understand the role that alcohol had played in my life, how it eased my anxiety, lulled me to sleep at night, and became my go-to at the end of the day.

I promised myself I wouldn't drink as Mom left this life. I would not drink.

When I'd arrived my sister Colleen had tried to rouse Mom from her semiconscious state. "Mom, Maura's here." She touched Mom's shoulder, as if this would bring her back.

I moved in close and held her hand.

The shiver of one eyelid, then another. She squinted at me, scrunched her face, said, "Your hair looks funny." Then she closed her eyes.

I laughed. She was right. My hair was cut so short it looked strange even to me. Leave it to Mom to say something about it. Not "You're here" or "I love you," but "Your hair looks funny."

I took a step back. The painting of the Sacred Heart hung over her bed in the girls' bedroom, the sword through Jesus' heart, blood dripping from a circlet of thorns on his head. There was a crucifix on the other wall. Jesus dying in agony. I didn't feel at home here anymore. To quell my fear, I bought more M&Ms and, after I sat at her bedside, I devoured the sugar.

Grief had brought me to this house. I sank into the

mahogany chair at the kitchen table with its yellow daisy oilcloth and matching curtains. It was December in the Bronx and wind seeped through in spite of the closed windows. The house smelled like cigarette smoke with a trace of coffee. I stood up and walked back to the girls' bedroom. Jo Anne looked up, nodded, and left. I sat and felt Mom's wrist for a pulse—weak, but still there. I looked at her eighty-three-year-old face and sunken cheeks. The wet cloth I held to her lips wasn't enough to hydrate her, but holding it comforted me. Colleen came in, sighed a long outrush of breath as if she'd failed Mom, her best friend. My mother twisted a tissue into an amorphous shape, a knotted thing that helped no one. But maybe it helped her. Colleen traded places with me, and she and Jo Anne worked to turn Mom over.

I walked through the room where my four brothers stared at the TV, their eyes glazed over. I walked back to the kitchen and the half-empty bag of candy. Later, I heard my brother Frank reading to Mom from a book, *The History of Sligo*. When I returned, her hands were over her ears as if the words were too much. He put the book down, glanced at me, and left. My other brothers rotated through as the TV babbled in the background, slipping from one show to the next, with commercials insisting that we buy their products.

Later, I called a friend who said, "Look at the seventh chakra at the top of her head. You may see a purple glow as she gets ready to leave."

Mom's gray hair was still wavy, as if with a quick brush she'd be on her way to a Sodality meeting at church to honor Mary. Hours later I saw it—a small flame of purple at the crown of her head. *Almost time*, I thought. Then out of the corner of my eye, as if the chakra had opened to another dimension, the flutter of tiny wings, several little ones appeared, like Tinkerbells, surrounding her head. My shoulders relaxed and I breathed easier knowing that she would have company on her journey.

Me, who'd spent nine years in the convent, praying to a God I barely knew, saw fairies and Tinkerbells? My life had brought me to believe in the sacredness that flowed in all of creation. I knew that these images were a sign of that sacredness, of all that is holy.

I told no one what I saw. I was grateful for this momentary vision, to this opening into the unseen world. I wanted to keep the experience close to my heart and prayed she would die in peace.

And she did.

We followed the rules that required us to call the police to confirm that the death was from natural causes. As I waited, I continued to craft a PowerPoint presentation on what to do in the case of pesticide poisoning ... *insecticides ... organophosphates ... chlordane ... malathion ... atropine ... antidote ... twitching ... excessive salivation.*

I returned to Mom on her bed. No more angels, no more purple flame. We waited for the police who came and sat in the kitchen with brother John who regaled them with tales of his escapades in the Bronx. I stared at the TV screen and listened as John entertained them. At one point they laughed so loud their voices echoed down the hall. I clenched my fists. How dare they laugh while Mom lay dead in her bed? I took a breath and let it out slowly. We waited for the medical examiner to tell the police they could release her body. Hours later, the call came, the police left, and we called Park Abbey Funeral Home.

Soon, two men dressed in black slipped Mom's body into the body bag. As they pulled the zipper up, my heart cracked open. I thought of the things I'd never get to say. All the things she wouldn't get to say to me. Kathleen, who had emigrated from Ireland, married fourteen years later, had seven children in ten years and was worn down by it all. Confounded by me, the daughter who had married God, then left the convent to move across the country. How she choked out "I love you" at the end of our phone calls.

And me, after years of therapy, finally able to say, "It's all right, Mom." I knew she had done her best.

My sisters and I led the men down the hall as the stretcher squeaked across linoleum floors that Mom so often had cleaned with ammonia. As we opened the front door and they rolled her onto the porch and down the brick steps, Mom's words rang in my ears: "They'll carry me out of here, feet first." No onlookers, just me. And my siblings. Stunned by it all. We watched them pull away, taillights disappearing out of view.

Those M&Ms saved me, stalled the gut-wrenching free fall as I chewed each fistful, the yellow, red, green, brown, trying to fill the hole inside me. As if I was looking for salvation. All of it dissolving into mush in my mouth and down my throat. *No alcohol*, I repeated to myself. *No beer or wine, no bourbon, no Irish whiskey. Save me*, I pled to the waves of candy I gobbled down in those hours.

◇

PARK ABBEY FUNERAL HOME smelled musty, its carpet replete with faded roses. Lysol failed to hide the decay. Mary, the owner, who reeked of cigarettes and beer, had painted my mother's fingernails pink, and pulled Mom's hair into tight curls.

I held myself together during the wake and funeral, through Cousin Bridie's scones and Irish soda bread, Domand Deli Italian cookies, and coffee from Mom's electric percolator that poured out streams of Maxwell House.

Then all was quiet. The company had left. My sisters and I sifted through Mom's closets and drawers, tucked her lamb's wool coat and house dresses into bags. We found over a dozen pairs of Sunday shoes still in boxes in the cellar waiting to be worn—black, white, beige, navy blue.

I still didn't drink.

Don't think about Mom, about how it will be. I forced my eyes away from her half-full coffee cup still on the stovetop.

When I returned to Portland, I fell back into my old routine. Work. Drink. Sleep. Repeat. I was lost in a haze of alcohol and grief. I managed to work another year before I quit drinking. I'm not sure how it happened. I only remember feeling so low I knew I couldn't keep doing what I was doing.

nineteen

BLOOM

WHEN I WAS seven, I told my sister Jo Anne a story as the sun pasted our sweaty bodies to the floor of Dad's Chrysler on the way to Rockaway Beach.

"A man jumped out the window and broke his leg," I whispered, pushing my brother John's smelly sneakers out of the way. Three brothers and my older sister got to sit in the back seat, but I was in my favorite private space, sitting on the floor.

Jo Anne stared, mouth open, like a baby bird waiting for worms. She said, "More. Tell me more." Her freckled face scrunched closer to mine.

I was hooked. At seven, I started to tell stories. Decades of notebooks piled up as I moved across the country. Then, after years in Portland, when I fell into a deep depression and started drinking more and more, the flow of words had stopped.

That lasted for years until I saw a print in a gallery and couldn't pull my eyes away. The ache to express what I felt cut through me.

Bloom by Tetsuro Sawada.

I went home, drank tea, went to bed, got up, went to

work. Day after day after day, the image of that print came back and so did the need to write. *Bloom*—dove gray bleeding into azure, into charcoal, into inky black, before a sunset red, next to gray. A lighter line above scarlet, pale yellow returning to charcoal. The end of something, the beginning of something, layers that embodied what came next. Who I was. Who I was becoming.

I returned to the gallery, bought the print, took it home, sipped tea, stared at it and wrote, one thought leading to the next and the next until I knew what I had to do.

⟡

I'LL DIE WITHOUT *alcohol.* The words were like a whisper, but clear, unmistakable, rising inside me.

The words "I have a problem. I think I'm an alcoholic," still lingered in the air after I'd told Barbara, my therapist, about my drinking, about the nights I spent alone, drinking more and more. As I talked, her eyes focused on me with this new revelation. Why hadn't I shared this over the many years of seeing her? Because I'd learned the habit of secrecy, of keeping my shameful addiction to myself. I knew that alcoholism was a disease that I shared with several family members. That didn't make me feel any better about it. If anything, I felt worse. I was too smart to be an alcoholic.

Or so I thought.

I thought of Uncle Jimmy, Aunt Maggie's husband, who had pushed his cousin over the railing after he'd had too much to drink. I didn't want to be like him or another alcoholic uncle who died after he fell in the bathroom. In the 1960s, folks like Mom refused to speak of the anguish of having an alcoholic family member. Their Catholic upbringing told them to offer up their suffering, to pray for relief. Therapy and counseling weren't an option. But I wasn't them. I was desperate to stop the shame of my alcoholism from taking over my life.

My therapist looked at me. "Can you pour what's left of your alcohol down the drain?"

I stared past her to a photograph of sunflowers on the far wall, their sunlit clarity a contrast to the shame I felt. Something opened inside me, as if my admission had revealed something else. Was it hope?

"Yes," I told her. Then I heard those words in my head, *I'll die without alcohol.* I didn't analyze them or wonder if I would really die if I stopped drinking. I felt chills, as if something bigger was at work than the feeble "Yes" I'd uttered. Maybe the voice was my fear, the old habit of shame and secrecy, rising inside me.

My therapist was the only one I told how, over ten years, my drinking had progressed. At Berkeley I had shared a bottle of cheap brandy with a roommate and, years later in Portland, I sat in my house alone, shades closed, sucking down glass after glass of wine. Good wine, I reasoned, so it wasn't so bad.

After brandy, I'd discovered Courvoisier. Then I graduated to flaming Spanish coffees served by tuxedoed waiters at Huber's in Portland where they specialized in pouring ingredients from a point high above a flaming glass.

"Well, now," I'd often say to my favorite mustachioed waiter, who'd poured dozens of these flaming masterpieces for me. "Didn't you promise you'd teach me how to do this?" The owner looked on from the entry way, taking in the good-natured kidding fueled by alcohol. In those days, I had fun with friends and loved the drama of that fiery drink.

Jameson Irish Whiskey followed. Bushmills would do if Jameson's wasn't available. My friends ordered their lighter-weight drinks, and I had mine. When I was with them, I didn't have more than one or two drinks, telling them that any real Irish-Catholic should drink Irish whiskey. They never guessed I had a drinking problem. Then there were years of vodka martinis with Stolichnaya, then Rusty Nails and gin and tonics. I swore off Guinness stout since I worried about calories, so I switched to other brands of beer—Heineken and Dos Equis with lime. Budweiser was my go-to when all else failed. Then came the wine years.

But nothing was ever enough. I always craved more and realized that the less my friends knew about how much I drank, the better. If I drank at home where I lived alone, no one would know my secret.

Leaving the convent decades earlier had opened new chapters for me—friends, jobs, and amazing adventures. I had no idea that it would also lead me to a point where I'd face my inner demons. I didn't drink in the convent. The compulsion to drink lasted for a decade after the stress of graduate school and a new career pushed me to my limits. At first it seemed to keep anxiety and my lingering depression at bay. I had no idea it also kept me from telling the truth. I did my job and kept my secret. I felt relieved when I went home, closed the door, let down the façade and drank, pushing down the shame with each sip. I learned not to answer the phone on Sunday nights when I knew I slurred. I was afraid that the person who was calling would realize I was drunk.

Years earlier, I'd wandered the streets of Portland with hundreds of others to celebrate the opening of the new Performing Arts Center. In a martini haze, I'd balanced myself against a light pole as I watched a trapeze artist walk a tightrope between the Arlene Schnitzer Concert Hall and the new center. I'd found a downtown bar and joined the throng, laughing, dancing, talking with passersby. I was flying high with the rush of being part of something bigger than me—street performers, music, dancing in the street, the illusion of being with others. But I wasn't. I was alone. My friends hadn't joined me. Perhaps I hadn't invited them.

I loved it all until I had to drive home. I sat for a while behind the steering wheel, then started my car and headed out. I think I avoided busier streets but I'm not sure. I was just glad when I made it home, parked, walked up the steps, fumbled the key in the lock, opened the door, and fell into bed.

I repeated this time and time again on weekends, without the fanfare of jugglers and trapeze artists, deadened by martinis, Jameson's straight up, or gin and tonics. It didn't matter as long as I had one, then two, then more, and more. Until I realized it was safer to drink at home and not drive. Sometimes I still met friends for a drink, but I learned to cut myself off early and, after pleading a headache, go home so I could drink more. The types of alcohol are almost endless, and I learned what worked for me. I was a quick learner. I loved the camaraderie between my drinking friends and me, the laughter that spilled out of darkened booths in the Virginia Café, the Veritable Quandary, or any number of downtown bars, often coupled with dancing at the Red Sea as reggae music blared over me.

I decided that wine was easier, favoring red, then switching to whites. Chateau Neuf du Pape for special occasions. I felt sophisticated. For a decade, I drank and told no one. I'd been in therapy during much of that time and was honest about my anxiety and depression but never about my drinking. When I answered "Yes," to my therapist, I could pour the rest of the alcohol down the drain, I forced myself not to think about what a waste it would be to do that.

But I knew I had to. My skin crawled with desperation to end the insanity.

That day when I got home from therapy, I stood at the kitchen sink, tore the seal off the last wine bottle, pulled out the cork, and poured it out. It wasn't quick. I held onto that bottle with two hands, my fingers blanched as I gripped it, afraid that if I didn't hold it tightly, it would fly up to my mouth. The aroma overpowered me, the sweetness, the warmth of fermented grapes. I salivated, remembering the comfort it had given me over the years. When the last slug drained out, I rinsed out the bottle, then opened the meeting schedule of Alcoholics Anonymous.

Don't think. Just go.

I regret that my uncles didn't get help.

I'm grateful that I did.

◈

IN 1993, I went to my first meeting of Alcoholics Anonymous and haven't had a drink since. More than three decades later, I'm still sober and I continue to write—about sunlight that slants through my window and reflects the radiance that is *Bloom*.

I think about my mother, the shoes she bought on sale, kept for a time that never came—the one extravagance she allowed herself, her own muted rainbow hidden in the cellar. I think about how she did her best to raise me and, along with Dad, showed me how to work hard. The stories they never shared with me motivated me to tell my story so life could expand, so I might become the woman I wanted to be, one whose secrets became stories, a woman who finally was at home in her life.

⋄

ONCE I STOPPED drinking, I heard my inner voice more clearly. I began to trust myself and my instincts. The questions about who God is and who I am in this world stay with me. One thing I do know is, if I stay sober, I can ask for help from others and from the spirit inside me. I believe my inner spirit wants me to be happy. The lessons I've learned along the way show me that asking for help is crucial. And that there is more to this world than I can ever understand.

The voice I'd heard as I prayed at Mrs. Wojtow's coffin and the one that shouted *"NO"* when I'd shaken Jonathan's hand, told me there was more to my inner spirit than I had ever realized. The Tinkerbells that surrounded Mom were an opening into the spirit world. I would not have heard or noticed these signs if I had been drinking. The clarity of their message hit me hard and changed my life. Thanks to these signs, I left the convent; heeded the warning not to trust my boss in Tennessee; and to stop drinking.

I bloomed into a woman of courage and hope.

epilogue

FOR MORE THAN four decades, I've told stories about my life in live performances. Many of those stories are in this memoir. One of the themes has been my gratitude for the mentors in my life, the people who showed me how they overcame or coped with the struggles that they faced. I decided to share more about these remarkable people, to tell how they had helped me, how they'd embodied love, forgiveness, and compassion.

In 2019, I decided to honor three people in a one-woman show I called "The Potluck." Instead of telling stories about them from my perspective as I'd done in the past, I told their stories as if it was them, talking about themselves. As each person spoke through me, I hoped their stories would intersect and reveal the common threads woven through each of their lives. The performance centered around a fictitious potluck dinner and ended with each character sharing their experience.

I performed "The Potluck" performance over a dozen times and, after it, I shared a simple meal with those who had attended.

When I thought about whose stories I should bring forward for this performance, two people immediately came to mind—Norma Morigi and Hobert Story. Each of them had touched me deeply. Then, I thought, what about my mother? I was reluctant to tell her story. How well had I really known her? How well had I known any of these people? Something inside me motivated me to share some lessons I had learned from each of them.

In story, albeit through a fictional potluck, they could come together in a healing circle—one that might salve wounds suffered by each of them in this life. Their stories might also bring hope to others. Norma and Hobert's stories might open my mother, and me, to greater levels of love and empathy. I trusted myself to craft the performance in a way that would honor each of them.

Because my goal was to create a sense of community with the audience, I was intentional about where I performed. Several times I shared it in the intimacy of a friend's home. I also performed for a few select community groups. I'll describe one venue that stands out—the motherhouse of the Dominican Convent in Sparkill, New York.

I was invited to gather with the Sisters in the community room where once I had buffed linoleum floors and dusted shelves. When I lived there, I did not speak to the professed Sisters. Head down, I skulked along the corners, in silence.

This time, however, I stood tall, confident in my story, in the life that had brought me back to the motherhouse. I stood in the center of the room and looked out at my husband, Ken, and at dozens of Sisters, some I knew, some I didn't. Minnie, known back then as Sister Kevin Francis, along with my former sponsor, B.A., Sister Beatrice Anthony, had joined us, as well as several Sisters I had entered with.

"Welcome, everyone, to this performance I call 'The Potluck.' Today, you welcome me back to the motherhouse where, in 1967, I became Sister Kathleen Maura and, later, Sister Maura. Nine years later, after I left the convent, I carried our shared spirit of helping others out into the world.

"I'm here to tell you about three people who are close to my heart, people who've had a major impact on my life, who've taught me about love and forgiveness, about trust and hard work. They are my mother, Kathleen, and my friends, Norma and Hobert. None of them are alive today, but the lessons they taught me helped me become the person I am now—a woman who is at home in her life and in the world.

"Before we begin, I invite you to think of someone who has been important in your life, someone who has had a major impact on you. Perhaps they are still alive. Perhaps they have died. Remember their face. How they laughed. How they smiled. Perhaps you were lucky enough to hear their stories. I encourage you to bring them into this circle today so that their memory is with you as I share the story of three people who were important to me."

I remembered my mother, Norma, and Hobert, and asked them to be with me as I brought their stories forward. I focused on the audience. One Sister in a habit and veil sat to my left. She looked at me and nodded, rosary beads draped around her hands. In front of me, another Sister—that one in regular clothes—moved her lips as if she was in conversation with a loved one. A deep silence surrounded us as memories filled the room.

And so, I began. As the stories of my mother, Norma, and Hobert unfolded, so did the themes of trust and betrayal, love, and forgiveness. I forgave my mother and wrapped her in love. My very presence there, in the motherhouse, had brought me full circle as I celebrated these mentors in my life and the lessons I'd learned from them. I spoke loud and clear about my journey as a woman who had withheld her voice to the woman I'd become.

I am Maura Bridget Clare Doherty—daughter of Irish immigrants and a descendent of the ancient Celts. I listen to my inner voice, speak my truth, and cherish the lessons shared by the mentors in my life, lessons that have helped me find home.

acknowledgments

THIS BOOK IS the culmination of many years of life, love, and learning to trust myself and others. I am deeply grateful to my husband Ken Demo, for his unwavering support; for Beatrice Dionisio (the former B.A.) who sponsored me into the convent; the two writing groups that have shared this journey with me: the Writers' Table: Dede Montgomery, Shelly Parini-Runge, Emily and Michael Wood, and Leigh Freeman; and my decades long writing partners: Ann Dudley, Sulima Malzin, Patricia Rimmer, and Marty Katkansky, as well as Nancy Day and Mim Mimmack, whose spirits live on.

So many have supported me, listened to my stories and read my work, and helped this book come to life. They include my sister, Jo Anne Doherty, Holly Greenfield, Minnette Duran, Thalia Zepatos, Mary Celnicker, and Judith Ervin. My thanks to Mary Bisbee-Beek who introduced me to designer Kris Weber and the staff at White River Press: Linda Roghaar and her team (including the fabulous copy editor Jean Stone and proofreader Janet Blowney) whose talents brought this book to life.

To all my many mentors: thank you for your kindness along the way.

Milton Keynes UK
Ingram Content Group UK Ltd.
UKHW020936160924
448404UK00014B/883